The GOLD DIGGER'S GUIDE

How to Marry the Man and the Money

IVANA B. RICH

KENSINGTON PUBLISHING CORP.
http://www.kensingtonbooks.com

DAFINA BOOKS are published by

Kensington Publishing Corp.
850 Third Avenue
New York, NY 10022

All Kensington titles, imprints and distributed lines are available at special quantity discounts for bulk purchases for sales promotion, premiums, fund-raising, educational or institutional use.

Special book excerpts or customized printings can also be created to fit specific needs. For details, write or phone the office of the Kensington Special Sales Manager: Kensington Publishing Corp., 850 Third Avenue, New York, NY 10022. Attn. Special Sales Department. Phone: 1-800-221-2647.

Dafina Books and the Dafina logo Reg. U.S. Pat. & TM Off.

ISBN 0-7582-0660-7

First Kensington Trade Paperback Printing: October 2004
10 9 8 7 6 5 4 3 2 1

Design by Leonard Telesca

Printed in the United States of America

Contents

Preface

Go ahead. Admit it. You've pondered life on the other side of the fence. You've secretly flipped through some society magazine and wondered, just for a split second, what life would be like for *you* if you had a seemingly endless supply of cash. You've thought about how great you'd look in one of those deliciously expensive designer gowns. You've even committed that green-eyed sin. (Gasp!) You've felt a twinge of envy when you've seen or been in the company of someone you've perceived as having more money than you. Yes, you know it's wrong to covet thy neighbor's wife. Forget the wife! You just want her life. That's what I'm going to help you get.

First things first, let's do away with the term *gold digger.* Let's just remove it from our vocabularies. It has such an ugly connotation despite the fact that the actual definition really is not negative. The original gold diggers of the 1840s worked every day and took care of their responsibilities. They simply saw an opportunity to live a better life, and they grabbed it.

The promise of that new life was not as simple as it seemed. Remember, this was a time long before our modern conveniences like planes, cars, and trains. The way for Easterners to get to San Francisco was quite arduous, and in lengthy, cross-country wagon rides it could entail a boat trip down the East Coast, around South America, past Mexico, and back up the West Coast until San Francisco was in their sight. Then, once there, wily businessmen bilked them out of tons of money, charging them $100 for a meal or $15 for an aluminum pan to sift through the sand until, ka-ching, gold dust.

So understand that it was difficult work getting to such a place, and once there, these gold diggers had to fight to hold on to what was theirs. Naysayers balked, regarding these treasure seekers as lazy wishers who were unwilling to do the real work it took to attain success. But ladies, I know that you've put a lot of work into ventures that just didn't pan out. You've wished, prayed, and shaken that aluminum sifting pan of love more than a little bit only to find out that you didn't even have gold dust there. You ended up with a pile of rocks. I want to help you change your prospects. I want to help you get on the path to the life that you're supposed to have.

But what we must do first is to just drop the phrase *gold digger* from our lexicon. Let's replace it instead with Greatly Determined, or Glorious Diva, or even Goal Oriented and Driven because this is a goal. You do have an end point in mind, and believe me, the finish line is closer than you think. So let's get on the path, shall we?

One more thing: Before you set on the path, remember that you should always marry for love. That is imperative, as you will stand before God and man professing your love for someone. Just remember to fall in love where money is. Okay, let's go.

Author's Note

Despite what you will read in the personal tales that I recount, please know that I married for love. My dear husband of seven years is the other party in the most precious relationship I have. Any stories that you will read about trysts gone bad or former flings are just that, stories from history. They are in no way attempts to recapture feelings of old, and they should not be interpreted as such. My husband is my heart, and our love is built on the solid foundation of the Rock, not man's foundation of finances.

The GOLD DIGGER'S GUIDE

TAKING INVENTORY

I once had a friend whom I'll call Paula. Paula was an attractive young lady whose heart was good. She had studied for a year and a half at a junior college. Because of limited finances, Paula didn't feel as though she could continue her education, so she dropped out of college and found a job as a receptionist in a medical practice. She met a young man who was a few years her junior, and they began dating. He was a college student from a very moneyed family, and his parents provided him with a late-model car, and they bought him a house to live in while he studied at an urban campus. Though Paula was bright and funny, she would often become enraged with her boyfriend over simple matters that are a part of any college student's life. At the core of her fits was insecurity. She not only felt insecure about being a little older than he, but also felt inadequate about her comparative lack of money and the lack of closure in her education.

One day during a heart-to-heart with me, she revealed her sentiments. As a member of a popular fraternity, Paula's boyfriend garnered a great deal of attention from young ladies in the fraternity's auxiliary organization, sorority women, and other women on campus. For example, one night he and his frat brothers were throwing a shindig. As a host of the party, he worked the room, circulating to make sure that every glass was filled and every foot was in motion. In between greeting guests in attendance, he popped over to chat with us, and when he did, he was sure to give Paula some public display of affection. Rather than feel soothed, she seethed when one female reveler hugged him a little longer than Paula liked. Even after he pried himself away from the young woman, as he pointed to Paula in acknowledgment, she was still incensed, and she let him know it. After an embarrassingly heated discussion with him on the front steps, she asked me to drive her home.

On the way to her house, I let her know that I thought she had overreacted. She began venting, saying that she was tired of feeling disrespected by him and those floosies who were constantly throwing themselves at her man. After listening to her tirade, I interjected, saying, "Well, if you're that concerned, you certainly don't leave the party with your turf unprotected." Grasping my point of view immediately, she ordered me to turn around and take her back to the party, where she spent the rest of the evening playing chicken with any woman who looked in her man's direction.

At the root of Paula's problem with her social butterfly/ junior executive were insecurities about how she measured up to the other women in his circle. Paula complained that these women were smart and attractive, and their parents could afford to send them to a prominent four-year university while her single mother had not been able to. She wasn't savvy enough to know that grants, scholarships, and loans could have financed her education, so her feelings of anxiety and jealousy were heightened. In despair, she turned to me and asked if I would feel the same way if I were in her situation.

Distance tends to make us more confident, so since this wasn't my relationship, I was able to give a moderately objective opinion. I clearly saw what she needed to do.

"Honey," I said. "Rather than feel badly about his constant interaction with other women, make sure that your game is tight. He is a friendly person, and he loves his frat, so he's going to continue to socialize with a lot of people. Some of these people will be college-educated women who happen to look good. In addition, he's going to have study sessions with female students from time to time. Don't sulk about it. Instead, stay in the game so that the two of you can remain on the same team."

I would love to say that Paula and her man formulated a solid game plan, and that they're still playing on the court of love. Unfortunately, that's not the case. She let insecurity get the best of her, so Paula missed out on a great guy. The ultimate fumble of the game was that he came equipped with a pretty hefty wallet.

I want us to examine Paula's predicament. Sure there are probably things that her boyfriend could have done to assuage his woman's fears. That, my friends, is a different book. It is my belief that because Paula didn't feel good about where she was, she deflected that negativity onto her man. His every conversation with another woman was flirtation. His every study group was an affair waiting to happen. Instead of worrying about what the other women had and what she was lacking, she should have been trying to bring herself up to speed. She was fit and attractive, so there really was no room for improvement there. But there were other areas where Paula could have used a makeover. Since her boyfriend was a business major, auditing a course or two in his major would have broadened the scope of their conversation. She might have also picked up and read a few biographies about interesting business leaders. In addition to impressing him with her knowledge, she would have also demonstrated her willingness to try to be versatile. As for getting over the insecurity that plagued her interactions with his female collegiate counterparts, she might have tried to strike up a conversation with a few of them. Getting to know them and their motivations sure beats guesswork. Besides, she could have learned a thing or two. Sure, Paula's lack of a college degree might have been symbolic of other feelings of inadequacy, but at least with a degree in hand, Paula would have had one less thing to worry about. If her own canvas had been filled, she would not have been worried about what was sitting on someone else's easel.

Understanding that metaphor is key in getting and keeping any man worth his salt. Many of these Money Men are quite powerful, and handling insecurity is not high on their list of priorities. That means that you, dear sister, have to come correct.

What does it mean to come correct? I'm glad that you asked. It means that you must be able to hit the ground running when you find a man whose persona and pocket fit your profile. Know who you are. Know your strengths and weaknesses. Know what needs work, and know what your assets are. The one factor that is certain is that honesty in your self-assessment is vital.

Men give us clues all the time about what they like in women. We, however, have found it difficult to conform to their desires for a number of reasons. In some cases, we've found their goals quite difficult to reach. Sure, it's easy to look as glamalicious as actress Jada Pinkett Smith if you've got a stylist dressing you and a makeup artist painting you to perfection. Most of us don't have that . . . yet.

In other cases, we've got too many balls up in the air, leading to a fierce juggling act that would shame any circus performer. I know how hard it is to be superwoman all day and "Lolita" all night. The whole thing can be grueling. That's why it's important to simplify. Once you've cut back, you can put your best foot forward and lead yourself to the luxurious life you'll love.

As noted earlier, honesty is important when taking inventory. The easiest way is to divide yourself into two parts. Those parts are mind and body. Because examining the body is easiest, let's start there.

Let me begin with myself. Nineteen was a fabulous year for me. I was a sophomore in college, and I was gorgeous. Plain and simple, sistah-girl had it going on. Over the summer before my second year, not only had I shed the "freshman fifteen" that comes as a result of trying to adjust from Mamacita's "mano-made" meals to Cafeteria Connie's answer to cuisine, but I had dropped an additional fifteen for good measure. I set foot on campus at 124 pounds, which, incidentally, was one pound more than I weighed in the ninth grade. Donna Richardson had nothing on me. I was so disciplined that I worked out if I even thought about sweet potato pie. I remember this one piece of workout machinery that I used in the gym. It reminded me of medieval gynecological stirrups. Torturous it was, but after one session in it, my stomach was as tight as a Ghanaian drum. My gams were etched with delicately carved muscles. As for my boobies and my bum, I nicknamed them "The High" and "The Mighty." Now that you have a visual image of how my body looked, you really need sound effects. Imagine firecrackers. (Pow! Pa-pow-pow! Pow!) Yup, that was me.

Along with this "renewed" body came renewed interest. Fellow male students who had grown comfortable in friendship with me began sniffing around me like pooches that had just unearthed a bone they'd buried and forgotten from last fall. It was all quite amusing, but the sensitive side of me whispered, "I'm the same person I was thirty pounds ago." That's not what they saw, though, so I learned that appearances do count.

In addition to attention that I got from college guys, I noticed a new breed of gentlemen casting glances in my direction. Many of them were thirty-somethings, and they frequented the jazz clubs, health food stores, and other establishments that I happened upon in my travels. By a stroke of fortune, most of them were well off and fairly nice looking. I saw what they had to bring to the table, and they saw "The High" and "The Mighty." I made a few connections with some of these potential Money Men, but these trysts were short-lived for reasons I'll reveal a little later.

Some of us may have to do a little more work to retrieve those nineteen-to-twenty-five-year-old bodies, but believe me, it's worth the work. Not only will you feel good, but you'll look "mahvelous," dahlink, and your potential Money Man will see it as well. Some of us will be trying to whittle away post-baby fat (which reminds me . . . don't have any more babies until you've *married* your Money Man), and others will be cutting the comfort calories that we've accumulated. Whatever the source, ditch them. They're weighing you down.

Now this is not to say that big women can't be attractive. We certainly know differently. Star Jones is gorgeous. Big and Little Oprah are smashing. My grandfather, a Southerner, told me in one of my plumper times that I was as big, round, and pretty as an apple. And of course, there's that sharp sister from church who makes us say, "You'd better go on with your big self." All of these women are voluptuous vixens, and I take nothing away from them. Yet psychology plays a tremendous role in relationships.

I must admit that I've done no studies in this realm, yet simple observation tells me that most men like to be bigger than their women. Perhaps this notion correlates with some mandate imprinted on the male genes that tells them to protect those who are smaller than they. Whatever the rhyme, whatever the reason, it sure is nice to know that something (other than me) is telling my man to protect and cherish me. That's easier to do if I'm smaller. (Before you get your panties in a bunch and start burning bras, remember that I never claimed to be a feminist.)

Aside from the size and shape of the body beautiful, we need to keep our skin sweet and supple as we search for Money Man. It should go without saying, but some sisters get so busy that they need to be reminded that dry skin is a turnoff. Everything about you should be beautiful and picture perfect every time you leave the house, as you never know whom you'll meet when you're out and about.

Our paws are the third thing that men examine when scoping out the scene that is you. (Number one is the body, and number two is the face.) Sometimes they are checking out the hands to gauge marital status. Other times they look simply out of curiosity. (Think of Jerry Seinfeld and his aversion to the woman with "man hands.") Whatever the reason, your tips should be in tip-top shape. Depending upon the type of Money Man you are hoping to reel in, your nail style will vary. "Nail style. It's just dead skin!" you remark with mild alarm. I wish it were that simple, my fair chickadee. Keep in mind that you are trying to fit into his world, as he's the one with the money, remember? You'll look a tad out of place showing up at the Barristers' Dinner with "French" manicured colored tips that coordinate with your red gown. (You might get arrested because they'll think that you stabbed someone with those daggers.) And while you won't stand out in the same glaring way, you'll seem mighty subdued among the flashier musical moguls at the BET Awards with a professional-length true French manicure. So even though you're trying to get into Monsieur Money Man's Monde, you must do things that are comfortable for you. If it's not your style to wear rhinestone decorations on each finger, but that's what life in your potential Money Man's life calls for, begin your search anew. And do it quickly. Perky boobs have a short shelf life.

Pampering our peds requires special care, as they are generally ignored for two of four seasons. This is a major mistake because in the high life, jaunts to Jamaica and Hawaiian holidays not only can be expected, but can be the norm. That means that those tootsies will be exposed for all to see.

When it comes to feet, simplicity rules. A nice, clean pedicure goes a long way. A recent rage was the French pedicure. It's found a home among simply polished peds in the high life. Things get confusing when you combine wicked stomps with flashily polished feet. You don't want to give your Manolos too much competition now that you'll finally be able to afford them, so keep your tootsies tame and simple.

Hair is also important when putting one's best foot forward on the path to plenty. The way you treat your hair says a lot about how you treat yourself. The way you treat yourself says a lot about how you feel about yourself. Give off good vibes by giving your tresses the royal treatment.

I've always said that people often hide behind hair. I've never thought that was a particularly smart move unless you've got something on your face that might need a little camouflage. (Think Anna Devane from "General Hospital." That scar was a bit much to take in without preparation, so that cluster of waves came in quite handy for her.)

Conversations with various men revealed that many men prefer longer hair on their women. God can only tell you why. Now this comes as bad news to some women for numerous reasons. Personally, pixie coifs intrigue me. I truly prefer shorter hairstyles, but unless you're Halle Berry, that doesn't mesh with the trophy wife image that many men dig. What's a Glorious Diva to do? If you can't grow it, sew it. But tactfully, ladies, tactfully. Don't get your coworker's sister's goddaughter's cousin to do it unless she is a licensed professional. If you don't have the inside track (pun intended) on someone who can maximize your diva quotient at a fraction of the cost, go to a reputable shop and observe. (You'll find that observation is invaluable throughout this quest, and this one stage is no different.) I studied one Glorious Diva with a borrowed mane, and I found her to be so stylish that I inquired about her hairstylist. After a consultation with this dream-maker, I thunked down the $300 that transformed me from Anita Baker smooth to Viveca Foxy. It was an investment in myself, and it surely paid off. If weaves are not your style, consider microbraids à la Toni Braxton. Aha! You didn't know that those honey brown tresses were courtesy of Mr. Ed. Well, in any case, she wears them magnificently, so keep them in mind as another option.

There are some Money Men who consider less as more. Those generally tend to be older, more conservative men who appreciate inner beauty as well as outer beauty. Their Glorious Diva doesn't have to "glam it up" on the regular. For all of the low-maintenance Glorious Divas, consider this type of Money Man as the object of your search.

Teeth are also quite important as you get your physical appearance together. If you don't have a dental plan at your current place of employment, you might want to consider switching gigs. If that's totally out of the question, there are things you can do to whiten and freshen; however, nothing takes the place of a visit to your tooth tech. Think about it. The Spice Girls were a really big deal a few years ago because we were all shocked that Great Britain had fine women with nice teeth. Aside from Downtown Julie Brown and Elizabeth Hurley, we haven't seen too many Brits with cute chompers.

Even when you have a ton of money, people are unforgiving of bad teeth. In a relatively recent national political race, a well-to-do, high-profile politician was running for the GOP ticket. He was taking a lot of heat for one of his financial plans, but he was holding his own. His wife hit the campaign trails with him, and she spoke on at least one of the Sunday morning talkies. Nice woman. Intelligent woman. Rich woman. But, oy vey! Her teeth were so bad that I don't think anyone truly heard a word she said. The collective moan across some circles was, "Come on, if he couldn't scrape together a few dollars to send her to a dentist, can we really trust him with our tax dollars?" That just goes to show that even with oodles of 0s in your bank account, damaged dents can ruin you.

Aside from needing charming choppers to attract Money Man, your new life will put you in the public eye a lot more. Whether it's benefit balls or movie premieres, you're liable to be photographed a lot more than you are now. With that in mind, your image must reflect Your Royal Flyness.

Another thing to consider is getting one of the popular body-buffing techniques available at a day spa near you. One high-profile heiress remarked that after a weekend of treatments at one spa, her husband told her that her body was like a sixteen-year-old's, and that he couldn't keep his hands off her.

Getting the body together is the easy part. Getting the mind together takes a little more time because it's a lot more complex. Part of the mental adjustment is the process of undoing. It sounds simple enough, but it's pretty tough.

The other part of the mental adjustment is the act of building.

A young associate of mine whom I'll call Dina recently faced a minihurdle in the challenge of undoing. At eighteen, she had just finished a precollege summer session. In the brief time between summer school and the formal start of her freshman year, Dina and I went out to lunch. I drove to the shopping district surrounding a nearby Ivy League university. That simple act alone gave her goose bumps. Why not eat at one of the local establishments that we know so well? she asked. Because it's vital to venture outside of one's comfort zone every now and then, I replied. After lunch, we strolled the square, sticking our heads into chichi shops. Dina was nervous as we approached the Coach store. Ignoring her anxiety, I dragged her into the store. Once inside, she kept her hands down at her sides, as if an axiom from her childhood was set on repeat in her head. "Don't touch anything, Dina," it seemed to say over and over. Being the agitator that I am, I fingered every leather good in the store, and after each stroke from my delicate digit, I passed the piece on to her. I remarked on the fine craftsmanship to her, and she simply nodded her agreement. Upon exiting the store, I grabbed her hand.

"Honey," I said. "You have every right to be in that store. Your money spends as well as anyone else's. This is going to be your world, so you might as well get used to it. Claim the finer things. Put your name right on it, girl."

The maternal admonition that had been running through Dina's head was much more than a warning against squandering money. What her mother had unwittingly told her was that these things were out of her league. Though Coach bags were not really in the college coed's budget, they very well could be a part of her future reality. That's the point that I wished to impress upon her, and that's the point that I want you to get, as well.

Only you can define how much money is enough money for you. Only you can define the type of life that you'd like to live. Those choices are up to you, but know that abiding by your vow of a life of affluence is going to sometimes be difficult. It's always hard to stick to your guns with any decision you make, but this might truly be one of your life-altering tests.

My friend, whom I'll call Macy, always had champagne taste and a beer pocket. Raised by a single mother, Macy lived in a humble apartment. Her apartment complex was, however, situated amid a setting of opulence that was quite impressive. Macy, a pretty dark brown girl, attended high school with children of economic producers who seemed to be magnets for money. She immersed herself in school activities, and combined with strong academic achievement, her well-rounded nature earned her a scholarship to college. After graduation, Macy began dating a young man who aspired to be a doctor. Macy worked around her boyfriend's medical school schedule, playing the devoted girlfriend. He saw all of the support she was giving him on his quest to become a physician, and he knew that she would be the perfect wife for him, so he proposed. Well, of course, Macy was thrilled, and of course, she accepted . . . with one hitch. They wouldn't tie the knot until after he finished medical school. In the meantime, they would still date, and she'd still be supportive when and where she could, always retiring to her own apartment for the evening, of course. (Darlings, please know that the easier you make things for men, the more complacent they'll become, and they won't feel rushed to do anything, let alone make a proper lady out of you. So as the old saying goes, don't put the cart before the horse.) So on their wedding day, Macy became the wife of Dr. Blah-blah. Yes, he still had to complete his residency, but for the most part, the struggle was over, and she didn't have to get her hands too dirty in the process.

The difficulty here was in telling her fiancé to hold off until after medical school. Macy had already known struggle in her life, and she refused to have that kind of struggle in her marriage. I am quite happy to report that Macy's husband is now finished with his residency, and they have purchased a rather charming home. Their first child is nearing school age, and Macy is expecting their second child.

Not putting the cart before the horse is a really tough thing for many women because, by nature, we're nurturers. We like to make people happy, but in the process, we often sacrifice ourselves. Then, when the proverbial smoke clears, we feel like we're left standing alone. In order to combat this situation, we need to acquire a healthy sense of selfishness because that is at the heart of self-preservation.

That, my darling diva, is the thing that will help you to maintain your dignity and divahood when everything else seems to be crumbling around you.

I've never considered myself to be particularly conservative, but I think that a lot of us could benefit from looking back in time at the courtship rituals of our foremothers. So many things were simpler then, and often with simplicity comes clarity. Many, if not most, of our foremothers had fathers around who would not allow certain things, like shacking up without the benefit of marriage, because they knew the danger of allowing that to happen. Men know themselves, and sometimes what they don't know about themselves, we have to tell them, divas. The point is, with the disappearance of so many fathers from the home, women have to be strong enough to advocate for ourselves, putting our collective feet down when confronted with a situation in which we forecast that we might be compromised. We have to be unafraid and unflinching in our choices, and most importantly, we have to be observant. Countless examples of on again–off again relationships tell us that it's just too darn messy to move in with someone you're dating. Both parties are simply "playing house" without the commitment. Keeping in mind that nothing is guaranteed, it's much easier to walk away from a relationship that hasn't been formalized than it is to depart from one that has been. If you know that you have to answer for your actions, you're less likely to do something stupid. Adding children to that uncommitted mix just leaves one more person—the innocent, most vulnerable person—in a state of limbo-like instability. So just think before you make any decision that looks and feels like fool's gold. Divas, you know that the signs are almost always there. We just have to observe and pray that fortune is on our sides.

Suppose you're not as fortunate as Macy, with her recipe-ready rich guy. (Just add a little time, and presto, he's done!) That means that you will have to be direct and definitive with saying no to all of the frogs who come your way while awaiting your prince. I don't believe in the philosophy of kissing a few frogs before finding your prince. Doing things that way will get your lips all icky, send you to the dermatologist, and thrust you back to step one. Who needs that headache? Don't lower your standards as you are on this quest, or you'll sorely regret it. For proof of this, let's examine the case of Erica.

Erica was born with the proverbial silver spoon in her mouth. The granddaughter of a well-respected dentist and the daughter of a businessman, Erica grew up in a house peopled with servants and nannies. Erica fell in love with a promising young man whose eyes were fixed on a career in politics. They got married, and he enrolled in graduate school while she supported him financially and emotionally. Upon his graduation, he landed an internship with a promising politico, and after his yearlong internship ended, he began working as a legislative aide with the deputy mayor's office. While he gained a great deal of valuable experience and made a lot of important contacts, he did not make the kind of money that his wife had been accustomed to having. This, of course, was greatly disappointing to Erica, who, now with three sons, is living in an apartment on the edge of the posh end of town. With her husband working during the day and teaching political science a few nights a week, Erica is tasting a hint of her past life, but the taste is bittersweet because she can't fully appreciate the flavor.

On the other hand, Natalie never lowered her standards. The younger of two children, Natalie, too, enjoyed a life of privilege. The daughter of a judge and stockbroker, she never knew the meaning of the word *compromise*. She never had to because things always went her way. She was not a brat by any stretch of the imagination, for her parents would never tolerate that. She was intelligent and worked diligently in every task presented. Natalie attended a well-known women's college, and she met her future husband at the medical school of the men's college directly next door to Natalie's school. With parents as thorough and accomplished as Natalie's, her fiancé knew that he had to come correct. He did indeed. After beginning work as a surgeon, he proposed to her with a two-carat ring. Natalie was not surprised when the contents of the ring box twinkled before her eyes. In true BAP manner, she had made it known through words and actions that her standards were high. He rose to the occasion, and now the two of them live in moneyed marital bliss.

Like Erica and Natalie, you have an aim to live well. When you compare their situations, you can see that the lowering of standards, even temporarily, will result in aggravation. Again, why waste time? You know what you want, and you deserve it.

Let us continue. Our objective is to get you in the mind-set of life in the luxurious lane. The first thing to do is to see what "they" see, feel what "they" feel, and do what "they" do. Surround yourself in their trappings enough, and it will begin to feel normal.

Go to your local bookstore and cruise the magazine section. Search carefully for magazines that cater to people living the kind of lifestyle that attracts you. This is a little tricky because you, as readers, have diverse tastes, and the stations for which you are aiming are different as well. Just know that there are certain trappings that are standard, and they are regarded highly by all kinds of rich people. With that in mind, pick up copies of *Money, Black Enterprise, Town & County, Essence, Odyssey Couleur, Vogue, Elle, Ebony*, and *W*. Also pick up a copy of the locally published magazine catering to the affluent in your town. These periodicals will not only cultivate your mind, giving you a wide exposure to business and finance tips, but they will also show you quite a few toys and hideaways of the rich.

For example, *Black Enterprise* will not only sharpen your business acumen, but with its announcements of up-coming organizational events and magazine-sponsored summits, ski trips, and golf outings, you'll be in the know. *Money* will give you guidance about where to put your nickel, and it will give you a working vocabulary in fiduciary studies, which you will need on your way to becoming *and* after you've become Mrs. Money Bags. *Essence* will report on decorative trends, give fashion and beauty tips, bring you up to speed on social issues, and keep you grounded. *Odyssey Couleur*, a newly established magazine, will offer suggestions on vacation spots abroad and stateside. *Ebony* will show you other people like the future you: "statused" and established.

In the other magazines, I have found the advertisements as helpful as the articles. Through the ads, you'll become acquainted with the scents, the designers, and the baubles that adorn the rich. *W*, whose target demographic is a well-traveled, upper-class woman, will introduce you to the inner circle of the rich. You'll see them at the top of their game at galas and gatherings where they glitter like gold. *Town & Country* will display the well-designed abodes where the rich abide. Have a pen and paper ready to make note of the "it" affairs in major metropolises in the country. *Vogue* and *Elle* will take readers to the front row at couture shows. They will also tell you what the "high-enders" are reading, where they're eating, and what they're doing.

Once you have these savvy reads tucked under your arm, you must take the next step. You must enter one of the boutiques mentioned in the magazines so that you can familiarize yourself with the products you'll be wearing once you've struck gold. When you enter, be dressed well and be relaxed. You'll be surprised at how well you are treated in these establishments. No giddy high school salesgirls will bother you or stare at you blankly before trotting off to "go ask her mahnagerr" about some trifle. Instead, you'll be greeted by someone as well groomed as you are, who can answer your question with grace and ease. You might even be offered wine or hors d'oeuvres while you peruse in-store catalogs.

I must warn you. This pampered life is quite different from the drudgery to which you are accustomed. In my old life, I was lucky if I could make the snack machine work in the dingy lounge at the Dodge dealership. Meanwhile, while accompanying a moneyed old beau to a Ferrari dealership, I was escorted from the car and practically carried into a well-lit, well-ventilated waiting room, where I was served Perrier and I noshed on handmade dainties from a local bakery. It's no wonder that the rich always look so happy and relaxed while the rest of us look so harried and rugged. It's quite a mind trip, and you, future diva, have to be prepared.

In addition to reading the recommended magazines, you will be required to do some other reading to be up on your game. As you decide which road to riches you take, you will need to read material that will make you compatible with your Daddy Dinero. We'll address this point in more detail in the next chapter.

As you embark on this venture, just know that you are worthy of wealth. God wants you to prosper and live well. When you live well, you are more productive. When you live well, you are happier. When you live well, you are better able to fulfill your potential. So get to it, baby.

SETTING YOUR SIGHTS AND TARGETING YOUR PREY

So just how much money is enough money for you? That, my divalicious doll, is a question only you can answer. An annual salary of forty thousand dollars is fine for some, while others might think it piddly pennies. Sixty thousand dollars might seem sweet to some, but it could seem quite small to others. One hundred thousand dollars might seem like the top of the world to some, but others might think it the tip of the iceberg. Truly, it's your choice, and no one can decide but you.

I've developed a quick quiz to help you decide what dollar range might be right for you. With this in mind, you can see what type of diva you are, and what type of lifestyle might be conducive to your divatude.

1. On your first date with a potential prospect, you'd
   like to

   a. go to a movie then hit a casual restaurant.
   b. go dancing at a club frequented by flashy high-
      rollers.
   c. go to a casino so that you can see evidence of his
      monetary stash.
   d. spend an afternoon sailing before dining at a
      private club.

2. If given one thousand dollars by a beau, you would

   a. go buy that purse you've been dying to have.
   b. go on a shopping spree at Value City; a thou-
      sand dollars can buy a lot, especially if it's on
      clearance at a discount store.
   c. donate half to charity for tax purposes and buy
      some penny stocks with the other half.
   d. hold on to it because you know that a relative is
      going to hit you up for money sooner or later.

3. For a birthday present, you'd appreciate it if your beau

   a. sent you to the spa for the day.
   b. showered you with flowers and gifts.
   c. threw a surprise party for you and invited all of
      your peeps.
   d. surprised you with a beautiful puppy.

4. Your favorite type of dining environment is

    a. casual and comfortable.
    b. cultural and eclectic.
    c. chic and classy.
    d. country and cute.

5. Besides your church (because every diva needs to thank her God on the regular), clubs/organizations that are important to you are

    a. your sorority and other social organizations that may or may not have a community service thrust.
    b. tree-huggers and Puppy-lovers, Inc.
    c. civil rights organizations like the NAACP and the League of Women's Voters.
    d. any club with an open bar.

6. The kind of car that is most reflective of your personality is

    a. a convertible Corvette.
    b. a minivan.
    c. anything that's cute and reliable.
    d. a Range Rover.

7. The type of shoe that best depicts your life is

    a. a comfortable loafer.
    b. a stiletto.

c. a spectator shoe.

d. a trendy boot.

8. You view college as

a. a place to get your Mrs. degree.

b. a place to broaden your educational and cultural horizons.

c. a nonstop party.

d. a place where rich people send their kids.

9. Your ideal house would

a. have heat.

b. be a Tudor.

c. have plenty of space for your annual "throwdown" barbeque.

d. be a newly constructed or newly renovated model in a gated community or secured building.

10. When all is said and done, with the new wealth that you'll acquire, you will

a. use it to live well.

b. hold on to it; you've had more than one rainy day.

c. live frugally so that your kids will live well.

d. blow as much of it as possible.

Categorizing Your Answers

	Simone the Soccer Mom	Cheniqua the Chic	Sharon the Showgirl	Sasha the Socialite
1.	a	b	c	d
2.	b	d	a	c
3.	d	c	b	a
4.	d	a	c	b
5.	b	c	d	a
6.	b	c	a	d
7.	a	d	b	c
8.	a	d	c	b
9.	b	c	a	d
10.	c	b	d	a

Analyzing Your Answers

Question 1—First date

a. You recognize that there's time for building. Getting to know your potential mate first is important to you.

b. You like to have fun, and if people see you with your beau, that's an added touch.

c. You want to see exactly what kind of hand you're being offered. (You'd almost be less obvious if you were his bank teller.)

d. You know where the good grub is, and you don't apologize for having a discriminating palate.

Question 2—Thousand-dollar gift

a. You go for what you like, and devil be damned, you won't compromise. Thank the heavens for Sugar Daddies.

b. Aw, you adorable bargain-hunter! You've learned that your self-worth is not tied into a label.

c. You know money well, and you plan to keep it in your life.

d. You are family oriented, and you're used to "holding things down" from time to time.

Question 3—Birthday present

a. Sometimes, the best gifts are intangible, so the spa is perfect for you. You bond with other women-in-the know while there, and you recognize that with your newly toned skin, your real gift will come later.

b. You prefer to be the center of his attention all day. You think that demonstrates his devotion to you. Finding a diamond on your dessert dish would make a great finish to your day. That way, you'll have some great gifts to brag about to your friends.

c. Good friends and good times are important to you. You want people to eat, laugh, and dance the night away, but they better not track footprints in your house.

d. Sweet moments matter to you. It was quite thoughtful of him to get you this precious pooch, and you won't even mind walking it.

Question 4—Favorite dining environment

a. You like to be comfortable, and your food doesn't have to cost a lot. Besides, you can't get good chicken fingers just anywhere.

b. You are open-minded, and you appreciate creativity in cuisine and in life in general.

c. Your gigantic cz ring, necklace, and earring set almost blinds your date, but at least he can see how "clee-assy" you look in this expensive restaurant.

d. You can appreciate simplicity (and you think that Martha Stewart should be president, but that's a different story). Why not have fried chicken every once in a while? You can work off the calories by running errands.

Question 5—Important clubs and organizations

a. You share the wealth through service, but you know when it's time to be around "your kind of people."

b. You are so community-oriented because you want to make sure that those who come after you will benefit from your preservation efforts.

c. You are all about uplift, and you are in tune with history. You want the world to be safe for humans before you worry about whales and trees.

d. Need I say more?

Question 6—Car that reflects you

a. Flamboyance 'R' Us! You, like everyone else, know that a Corvette is expensive. You figure, why not show the world how much money you have?

b. Gotta get those kids around! At least yours is the model with the television and VCR.

c. You remember those days on mass transit, so you're not picky. Just as long as it gets you around, you don't care if the emergency break is a kickstand. If your wheels break down, you won't be completely stranded because you're resourceful, and you're not afraid of the bus.

d. You're a princess, and what better way to see your realm than from on high?

Question 7—Shoe talk

a. You've got to be practical. Smart shoes are the sign of a smart woman.

b. You think, the higher the heel, the better. If you've raised your boobs to his eye level, he'll be too distracted to notice that you're picking his pocket.

c. You figure that every lady who lunches should own a pair, though you're no mere spectator in life.

d. Always a funky fashionista at heart, you once saw Tichina Arnold wearing some on the "Keenan Ivory Wayans Show."

Question 8—Your view of college

a. You know that after college, your chances of finding someone suitable are slim.

b. You truly believe that what you learn in the ivory tower of academia might really be of interest. If not, you'll use the four years as a finishing school of sorts, and insert clever insight into intelligent conversation.

c. You think it's called "the yard" because there are so many boy-toys to play with. You are the one to whom the president of the university referred when he gave the "Look to the left, look to the right" speech.

d. You could hold your own intellectually while growing up, but no one showed you the ropes as far as the college application went. If given the chance, you'll go back at some point to get some closure.

Question 9—Ideal house

a. You're not that particular, nor are you savvy enough to form your own opinions about what's truly important for you in your abode. Whatever the style channel says, goes.

b. You like the classic style of a Tudor, and you'd prefer old and established to anything new.

c. Again, you've been without before, so it doesn't take a lot to satisfy you. In true "soul food" fashion, your house has the potential to become the family's gathering place. Just be sure to leave any sticky-fingered "cuuzins" right where they are because they will find their way back to rob one of your neighbors.

d. A palace made to your specifications is ideal, although you have no aversion to making modifications to an older home à la Simone the Soccer Mom.

Question 10—Money philosophy

a. You recognize that you can't take it with you, but you also know that spending needlessly is so "nouveau riche." You choose to have a good time being on "the scene," but you can appreciate kicking back with friends.

b. You might have been subconsciously scarred by an impoverished past, but you'll be okay. Your financial philosophy is a good one, but sometimes you can be a little tight with the cash.

c. You and your offspring will be well provided for because your Money Man recognizes that you and they are worth preparing for and protecting.

d. You don't prepare for a rainy day because you can't even see the rain with your head up in the clouds. You're the type who will wake up in the morning with nothing, so be careful.

Picking Apart the Profile

Simplifying the categories into four types of Glorious Divas is the easiest way to determine your lifestyle needs. Know that there may be some overlap because, after all, this isn't a precise science. Your roots definitely play into your spending habits, so while you might have Sasha's aspirations, you could have Cheniqua's sensibilities. You'll also note that, depending on your likes and dislikes, you'll enjoy some social events that fall outside of your category. Never fear. We're human, and we're subject to human inconsistencies. This is just a neat little way to decide where you fit, and how you should go about getting there, but it's not absolute, so don't sweat the Venn Diagram overlap.

SIMONE THE SOCCER MOM

Salary of potential Money Man	$100,000 +
Career of potential Money Man	White-collar professional (i.e., attorney, physician, sales rep, banker, engineer, professor/educator, prominent politician)

Simone, I've seen you all over. You've been a parent volunteer for special events at your child's private school.

With an expensive yet inconspicuous purse perched on your arm, you stroll casually through the cobblestone streets of the pricey shopping district. Bored with the stuffiness of the mall, you steer your minivan or Volvo wagon clear from it, opting instead for the much more serene setting of a tree-lined street. You prowl through the boutiques, recognized by some shop owners as either a regular buyer or a regular browser. As you search for trinkets to adorn your suburban home, you don't ignore the clearance or sales racks, although you could.

You do your own grocery shopping because you want to know what exactly goes into your families' bodies. Even your trip to the market is an experience when compared to most. Aside from the eat-in section where exotic dishes are served, cut, and warmed to your specifications, of course, you can sample just about everything in the store. Sure it's a little on the cher side, but would you do it any other way? Of course, you wouldn't.

Your house is spotless. Your contribution . . . a housekeeper who comes in a few days a week. At first, you felt a little guilty about hiring someone to do what your grandmother did with ease (while balancing two crumb-snatchers on her full hips and chasing another one out of her kitchen), but you soon forgot your guilt when you saw what was expected of you. Now you use that extra time that you would have spent cleaning on having your nails done instead.

Your furniture is a blend of Ethan Allen and great finds from High Point, North Carolina. It could be described as eclectically stylish. You've also included a collection of Lladros to which you add to every so often. Your art exhibit is extensive, and you're not afraid to include ethnic masks to the mix of artwork that adorns your walls. You've created a home that is both comfortable enough for your children to move about without fear and chic enough to entertain your husband's business associates. Your palace is perfect for you and your loved ones.

Education is important to you, as you are sure that someone a few limbs back on the family tree missed out on the opportunity to get "book learnin'" perhaps because of discrimination or some other tragedy. You've made it your mission to see to it that you and your children obtain at least a bachelor's degree. Your daughter may not use it because her marriage to a Money Man might not necessitate it, but you'd prefer that she's armed with a degree, just in case.

You've also insisted that your children are culturally refined with music, dance, equestrian, and foreign language lessons. Seeing that golf, tennis, and racquetball are the sports of business, they have those lessons, too. They are also members of children's clubs, like Jack and Jill, which performs service activities as well as introduces your kids to the children of other movers and shakers. They might find a future mate through their involvement in such an organization. Even if they don't, you simply want them in like company with people who value the same things you do. Not only are you children polite, but they recognize the impact of their actions on the family honor.

As for yourself, you pledge membership to a sorority while in college, and you are active in the graduate chapter of the organization as well. In addition, you hold membership in other women's groups such as the Links, the Continentals, the Junior League, the National Association of University Women, or the Girlfriends. You also make it a point to enrich yourself culturally as well so that you don't sound like an idiot when you entertain, which you do with ease and with relative frequency. You juggle all these things magnificently, and you manage to look dignified, collected, and gorgeous all the while.

Now that we've got a snapshot of your future, Simone, let's look at where you've been. You've come to the table with a meal of your own. You had to be able to communicate with your potential Money Man, so you stepped to the plate, degree in hand, armed for a new game . . . one of prosperity.

If you aren't fortunate enough to meet your future mate in college, don't fret. There are other alternatives. To catch your target, you have to do your homework. Find out where men like your potential Money Man would likely be. For you, sweet Simone, your Money Man was spotted at the following places:

Church
First Friday events (like the ones originating in
    Wilmington, Delaware)
The gym and outdoor athletic/hiking areas
Work

Citywide social events (like Chicago's "Taste of Chicago")
Cultural events (like Atlanta's Black Arts Festival)
Fraternity and sorority events (like Philly's Men Are
   Cooking)
Philanthropic events*

In addition, I again refer you to *Black Enterprise* and
Ebony magazine, which list events that your potential
beau may haunt.

Upon attending such an event, remember to look absolutely ravishing. I won't cite the statistics, but you know
them well. There are tons of women out there on the
prowl just like you. You have to find a way to distinguish
yourself . . . tastefully. That means L'il Kim pasties are out
of the question for you, Simone. Leave that to Sharon the
Showgirl. Of course, always have business cards handy,
and list your degrees behind your name. The more accomplished you are, the less a man thinks you need him for financial gain. Under the camouflage of self-sufficiency, you
can ease your way into his life and leather wallet. When
exchanging business cards, show interest, but don't seem
too eager. Even though you're hungry for the high life and
the man who can provide it, you don't want to seem
starved. Be gracious and witty, being sure to make an impression on him. Follow up with an e-mail or a note ASAP
to stamp your name in his memory.

Town and Country magazine regularly lists events that could use volunteers.
That's how you can avoid paying weighty ticket prices.

How do I stamp my name into his memory, Ivana? you ask. Good question. I'm glad you asked. To make yourself memorable, there must be a "thing" about you. What kind of thing? Anything. It can be a quirk of some sort, though nothing too strange, as you don't want to scare the man. You simply want to intrigue him. Your quirk could be something as simple as avoiding movies for which you've already read the book.

"You don't understand," you'll explain to him. "The movies very rarely stay true to the literary form, and I so cherish the written word that the corruption just about kills me." What a way to sound smart, huh?

Or a quirk that can be revealed as you get the ball rolling is that you're always a little late. He'll have to wait for you, and while he's waiting, he'll amuse himself for a short time, or you could give him something simple to do (i.e., program your VCR or check the speakers on your stereo). In those initial moments, he'll forget about you while he's tinkering with your toys. Once he's finished tinkering, his mind will return to you as you call out some witty anecdote while you're putting on the finishing touches. Just when he's about to get a little testy, you appear, looking ravishing, and in his mind, you're like a cool drink of water after a long hike. Ahh, refreshing!

Aside from quirks, you can achieve "memorability" by demonstrating your erudition. You know . . . showing off your smarts. Drop *un peu de français* into your conversation, and *voilà*, you look cultured. Then you can tell him that you picked up some French on your travels to Senegal the summer before you began graduate school. Or tell him that you studied French from the time you were four. Whatever the story, make sure that it's true because you don't want to start weaving a web of deception. Manipulation, yes, but deception, no.

So, after you've piqued his interest, and you're resting comfortably in your own abode, get to work. Go on the Web and see if there is any information you can find on your target either on Yahoo, Google, or some other search engine or his company's Web site. Also check local papers for any profiles that might be written on this man. In addition, research his field of employment, voraciously reading anything you can find about his company, the field, recent findings, or his competitors.

You can never underestimate how important it is to be a good conversationalist. We've already ensured that you are eye candy. Know that you need to be brain food as well. This brings me to the personal point that I mentioned earlier.

Again I return to that magnificent nineteenth year, the year that "The High" and "The Mighty" made their debut. After dinner with one of my prospects, we retired to his sprawling, spacious home, where we turned on soft music, and we danced in his basement that opened out to overlook his pool. When we tired of dancing, we sat on the supple Corinthian leather sofa, where I thumbed through a magazine. He was a thirty-six-year-old, second-generation doctor with several practices throughout the city. That should have been enough to make me churn out all kinds of questions. Instead, youthful inexperience left me tongue-tied, wanting for something to say.

"Have you ever been in a Chanel boutique?" he asked.

"No."

"You really should go. The clothes don't just hang there. They float on the hanger."

"Oh."

"Where's one place that you'd like to visit?"

"Someplace warm," I ventured.

"Like . . . ?" he probed.

"An island," I suggested weakly.

I could see the twinkle of interest dimming as his eyes moved from my face to "The High." I felt really bad because not only was I ill prepared to interact intelligently with this highly successful man, but I knew that he would automatically resort to my body as an "Oh, well." (As in, "Oh, well. At least I'll get laid this evening.") I had fumbled the ball, but that served as a lesson to me.

Even though I've fumbled a few times, there are numerous Glorious Divas who have held the ball high on their way to the goal, or should I say, gold. They've done it the Simone way, and they've made out like bandits. Let's look at the case of Donna for proof of this.

Donna is a "princess" in the upper echelons of her parents' social circles. Her grandfather had been a successful funeral director who passed down his wealth to his two daughters, Donna's mom and aunt. Donna's mom pursued a career in education, and she married an education administrator with a Ph.D. Donna was a member of an elite kids club, and she performed the debutante ritual as her introduction to society. After graduating from a private high school, she attended a fine college, where she pledged membership in a selective sorority. She enrolled in graduate school, and she began teaching after completing her undergraduate degree. One April, she met a young man, a member of a prominent fraternity, at an invitation-only boat ride. He was impressed with her "princess" ways, and she had made such a lasting impression on him that he proposed seven months later. The young man, a tenacious pharmaceutical sales rep in his late twenties, owned two properties. In addition, he had just earned a $25,000 bonus, which he socked away in preparation for keeping Donna in the lifestyle to which she was accustomed. Two years later, after an engagement party at which they pulled in a little over $3,000, Donna and her beau married in a wedding that was the social event of the season. The two were even featured in a nuptials section of *Jet* magazine. Their first home was built to their specifications, and shortly after they moved in, Donna took great joy in designing a nursery. Yup, they got pregnant soon after they married, and their first child was born within their first year of nuptial bliss. Interestingly, instead of serving as a nail in the road toward the good life, Donna's pregnancy actually solidified her marriage in that typical Simone way. Here's how.

Some men, when faced with the prospect of fatherhood, flip the script and run in the other direction. Those are irresponsible, dishonorable men, and sometimes they've been "trapped" by irresponsible women who attempt to keep men in their lives (sans marriage) by using a baby. Not only is that an irresponsible move, but it's a stupid one as well. It rarely works, divas, so don't do it. (Remember my admonition about not putting the cart before the horse. Far too often it's the baby who is left on the side of the road.)

Other men, when faced with the prospect of fatherhood, become almost Cosby-esque in their enthusiasm. This type of honorable man is usually responsible, and he often has a solidly successful career that pays well. (Please note, we all have a "cuuzin" who gets his kicks out of spreading seeds all over town like he's in a race against time. We're not talking about these baby-breeding bums.) If this enthusiastic father is not already married to the Glorious Diva, he will quickly stand before someone and profess his love for this woman so that he can make an honest lady out of her. His feelings of familial responsibility run so strong that he will gladly and happily provide for his wife, who is in a delicate condition. He'll work two jobs if he has to do so, simply to ensure their comfort and happiness. Donna's husband is that kind of man, which he demonstrated shortly after the birth of the baby diva. He didn't want Donna to return to work because he knew it would be beneficial for her and the tiny Divette to bond. After two years at home, she resumed her teaching responsibilities, but her return was short-lived as they became pregnant again. Now, two pregnancies and two houses later, twenty-nine-year-old Donna is still smiling as her husband's bonus checks are still rolling in.

Know that the road to the Glorious Diva lifestyle à la Simone can have twists and turns. Interestingly, the bumps along the way can show the human frailty in all of us, making the potential Glorious Diva look like she's in need of care. That is the case with the next Greatly Determined doll whom I'll call Jesse.

Jesse's mother was an educator, and her father was an attorney. Educated in private schools, Jesse was the epitome of a BAP, complete with braces and a Denise Huxtable flair for clothes. Upon graduating from a prestigious prep school, Jesse enrolled in a Southern college, where she intended to get her B.A. and her Mrs. degrees. Fun found her address, and she lived it up until a little mishap sent her home at the end of her freshman year. For her sophomore year, she enrolled in a college near her parents' home, and she commuted to classes daily. Unfortunately, this school didn't sit well with her either, so she left at the end of her sophomore year, and she began working in retail at a modish mall in a high-end business district. Impressive with her articulate speech and her panache, Jesse was quickly elevated to the position of manager in a new store in a suburban shopping square. As the manager of this enterprise, Jesse was called upon to see to it that the store was spotless. Her upbringing had not lent itself well to cleaning up after one's own messes, so Jesse's appointment was short-lived. She spent the next few years fruitlessly floating from job to job, yet she was enjoying herself in that erratic, indecisive, Denise Huxtable way. Quite the social butterfly, Jesse attended countless parties and social gatherings, and one evening, she found herself attending an event sponsored by a local chapter of a black professional club. There she met an architect who was about fifteen years her senior. He was smitten by her beauty and youthful vitality, and he found her vacillation charming and reminiscent of Holly Golightly from *Breakfast at Tiffany's*. They were married within two years, and he converted a warehouse that he owned into a fashionable dwelling for his hip, young wife. She became pregnant soon, and the groom was thrilled. Shortly after the birth of their daughter, the mature Money Man took his two princesses on a vacation to Monaco, showing his bride that she was his Princess Grace. Since then, she has opened a marketing business of her own, and their daughter is said to be quite the little lady, having benefited from the one-on-one time with Mom that a financially stable Money Man can provide.

CHENIQUA THE CHIC

Salary of potential Money Man	$250,000+
Career of potential Money Man	Musician, athlete

Cheniqua, girl, I've seen you, too. Your road has been pretty tumultuous, but now you stand, regal and fierce. You strut through the mall, eyes shielded by designer shades. Anytime the temperature drops below fifty degrees, you'll whip out your fur, and you make it look better than it ever did while it was living. You are what LL Cool J refers to as a "Round the Way Girl." Things haven't been easy for you, but you've persevered throughout with your spirit growing stronger with each setback.

Your upbringing tells you to be frugal, so you shamelessly peruse the aisles of the local Target; however, you are inclined to try out your newly minted credit card at Saks every once in a while. In decorating your home, you're inclined to go to a run-of-the-mill furniture store where you'll purchase furniture in preformed suits, leaving creativity, individuality, and personal style out of the picture in favor of convenience. Besides, your wavering level of confidence will not allow you to spend a lot of money on something that might look crazy in your new home. Cheniqua, your girls, or even your mother, for that matter, will talk you into buying goodies from Bloomie's where you're tempted to spend that $4,000 for a wooden kitchen table. In either case, your single-family dwelling is hooked, and you reign like the belle of the ball. Cheniqua, you have no problem hiring a housekeeper to tend the home front, but you'll very carefully keep a watchful eye on everything she does. You won't have her loafing around and trying to get paid for it. And you'll make sure that she doesn't linger too long over your children and that she rarely sees your husband. No other woman, especially an attractive one, who knows your husband's habits should see him on a regular basis. That leads to feelings of comfort and a sense of familiarity that might leave you, dear diva, out in the cold. Think about all of the secretaries who have "run off" with the boss. (Remember, there's no sense in relearning a lesson that has already been taught.) Trust me. I maintain veto power over the secretaries and assistants my husband selects for his firm, opting for "fluffier," seasoned women with British teeth. While it sounds like a lack of trust on my part, it's not. It's simply insurance that temptations aren't easily provided for my Money Man.

Cheniqua, back to you. Your taste in clothing is impeccable, as you have had plenty of time to scope out trendy duds in the fashion magazines scattered around the hair salon where you work. You are creative and talented, and you have no problem with wrapping a faux Louis Vuitton scarf around your torso and sporting it as a shirt. While your taste is stunning, you might lean toward what Simone would call G-Fab. After all, you admire Mary J. Blige and Faith Evans, but unlike them, you are not appearing in videos, so you might have to tone things down from time to time. You really do enjoy fashion, and you're likely to attend fashion shows sponsored by local designers. You also love shopping, but your remembrance of tougher times sometimes makes it emotionally difficult to splurge. So while you can be thoroughly enchanted at North Jersey's Short Hills Mall or suburban Philadelphia's Court at King of Prussia, you're more likely to whip out the plastic at New York's Woodbury Commons or a similar shopping enclave in another town.

To help you over some of the guilt that you may feel when it comes to spending, Ivana is going to offer some advice. While you should never do anything that is uncomfortable for you, remember that you have resources that many people lack. Why not enjoy them and spread the wealth? Buy for family and friends, or donate your knack for fashion to an organization that needs clothing for women who are entering the workforce after a hiatus (i.e., Welfare-to-Work programs).

You probably have a child who was born to you at the age of nineteen or twenty. Relations with his or her father are strained, so you try to keep him and his weak drama out of your life. You are fiercely protective of your little one, so you try not to let unstable forces, including family members, invade his or her territory. If that means barring visits from his or her father at times, you do it, but be mindful that this may be to your child's detriment, as the child needs to know her or his roots. Your child is well behaved, and you try to keep him or her busy with football and basketball leagues and camp in the summer. Education is important to you, too, but for whatever reasons, you weren't able to attend college. That, however, has no bearing on the seriousness with which you regard your child's education. With excess time on your hands, you will have room in your schedule to be involved in your child's education in a way that will ensure success. When it comes to preparing for college, you'll have no problem with calling on Miss Sadie from church because you once heard her mention that her godson's brother's cousin once attended junior college. You'll follow every lead because you value education, and you'll do what it takes to see that your child gets one.

As for your club memberships, you enjoy nonstructured activities, so sororities and other such organizations are not for you. You might even harbor a bit of bitterness toward women whose pedigree, education, and status enable them to join such organizations. Your life has been very different from theirs, and you feel like you've had to work for everything that you've gotten, while you view their experiences as having been far more comfortable. On one hand, you wear your battle scars like a piece of platinum bling, but on the other hand, you wish that things had been as easy for you as it has been for these clubwomen. You might call them "prissy prima donnas" in your mind, but you'd never let them see you sweat. Where you're from, that display would be construed as weakness, and strength is what you are prized for. (If you were older, folks would call you "Big Mama" because you know how to keep it together.)

Your husband is an athlete, so you might do some charity work with some of the other players' wives. As for other organizations, you might be a member of the parents' organization at your children's school. Other than that, you simply cherish time with your sistah friends. They are your girls who have seen you through your drama and trauma, and while they were happy for you for hitting the "jackpot" with Mr. Money Man, they still eyed him skeptically because of their devotion to you. You spend your time with them dining, shopping, seeing comedy shows, or just lounging by your pool. You might enjoy girls' night out every once in a while, and you even tried establishing a book club, but most of your cohorts aren't big readers, so the club flubbed. That's okay, you embrace your girls anyway, and you know that there are some things you can do on your own.

Cheniqua, because you are so attractive, you might actually meet your Money Man just about anywhere. You carry yourself with confidence, and men automatically know that you are a no-nonsense kind of gal. In fact, the one who has crossed you might sleep with one eye open for weeks because he fears your wrath. You've met men while vacuuming your car at the car wash, while dropping off clothes at the dry cleaner, or while cruising down the aisle at the auto parts store. None of these men will be your Money Man, though. You might find your potential guy while out at the club with your coworkers, on board a cruise sponsored by a DJ, or at a celebrity basketball game. Your beauty causes you to stand out while in high-profile places, and you never leave without passing out at least two business cards that your cousin whipped up on his boss's computer.

You've got a good heart, and you're fiercely independent. While that initially attracts men to you, it might eventually scare some away because they question their importance in your life. So while it sounds archaic, my advice to you is to tone down your independent nature while in his presence. He'll feel less threatened by a damsel in distress. That might sound like a lot to swallow for you, Cheniqua, because you think that your pride is on the line, but girl, you've always wondered what it would be like to have a man cater to you, so you soon get over it.

While making the transition from self-sufficient to "needy" was difficult for one of my acquaintances, it wasn't hard for her to go from woeful to wealthy.

Tonya and her three siblings grew up in a supportive home where both parents resided. Neither had high-paying jobs, but food was on the table every night. While in high school, Tonya, like her older sister, expressed an interest in cosmetology. Around the same time that she was beginning her studies to be a beautician, a local athlete who attended school with her before moving and transferring to a better district was being recruited heavily by college football scouts. Tonya began a relationship with him that continued while he attended college out of state on a football scholarship. While she visited him on campus from time to time, she made it clear that, while she loved him, she wouldn't tolerate creeping, nor would she play second fiddle to some "high siddity" college girl. Either she was good enough for him or she wasn't, she declared when she found an envelope containing lace panties and a phone number in his dorm room. To drive the point home, Tonya pulled away for a while, focusing her energy on her craft. Her jilted jock soon tired of meaningless flings with mindless freaks, so he crawled his well-chiseled body back to her. She took him back only after she had collected a few glittery trinkets from him as penance. After he was drafted by an East Coast NFL team, he married Tonya in a beautiful ceremony, and the two moved into a palatial home in a hidden suburban community. While some NFL wives busy themselves with charities, shopping, raising children, or even idleness, Tonya wouldn't feel fulfilled if she didn't work. After finding good schools and day care centers for their young children, she opened a salon, where two of her three siblings work. With plans of expanding the shop, Tonya and her Money Man will be on their way to reaching his goal of having $10,000,000. Tonya will be bling-blinging all the way to the bank.

SHARON THE SHOWGIRL

Salary of potential Money Man	$40,000–$70,000
Career of potential Money Man	Blue collar (i.e., police officer, sanitation worker, longshoreman, fireman, construction worker, toll collector, electrician)

Sharon, Sharon, Sharon. What can we say about you? You've been spotted a lot of places because, frankly, you're hard to miss. You've clip-clopped your way through shopping centers and malls, wearing impossibly high heels and an eye-catching outfit that's just shy of gaudy. For you, there's no such thing as negative attention. All that matters is that all eyes are on you. Because of your limited education, jobs that you have selected vary from the respectable (bank teller) to the outrageous (stripper). You're inclined to visit high-end stores, yet your outlandish behavior, characterized by talking down to the salesclerks, immediately identifies you as a social climber. You were raised with the false idea that to be rich, you must be heartless, so that thought runs through your mind as you yell at the waitress because the hot water for your tea just isn't quite hot enough.

You planned to climb up the social ladder with your looks, but you didn't quite have the skills to rope the man who could afford to give you life in the lap of luxury. Drug dealers were out of the question. First, while they boasted of deep pockets and drove flashy cars, they parked those hot rods right in the same projects in which you lived. Second, they seemed forever embroiled in danger. Third, that addicted relative was reminder enough of the trouble that dope peddlers wreak in our community. So they seemed hardly worth your attention and interest, but you did eye them and their multiple lady friends to see the latest fashion trends. And when you heard about the occasional hustler shutting down a restaurant for a night just to entertain his friends, you wished that you could divorce your conscience. Instead, you opted for a hardworking, blue-collar brother with a steady cash flow, a solid work ethic, and health benefits.

Your town house is a major step up from the apartment where you and your family were crammed for the first eighteen years of your life. It's decorated with leather and Italian lacquer because in your mind these things scream, "I have arrived!" Your artwork is of the framed street-corner poster variety with fake flowers affixed to the mirrors. To you, this is a step up from the framed picture of Martin Luther King and JFK that hung in the dining room of your family's apartment. You've collected knickknacks from Lenox stores in day-after-holiday specials. Never mind that the ivory-colored elephant is inscribed with last year's date. You simply turn that side out of public sight, and you admirably keep on steppin'. As television's Judge Mathis says, "You know how to make do." You do not have a housekeeper, so on the regular you do the best you can, performing the cleaning equivalent of a "hooker's bath"—cleaning only those places that are visible.

As for education, it's not particularly important to you. You never did well in high school, but it wasn't because you weren't smart. No one ever stressed the value of education to you, so you saw school only as a place to play and meet guys. While you would agree that a solid education is the basis for the future success of your children, you don't take the necessary steps to make sure that your kids do well in school, as that would take too much time. You're hoping to groom your daughter to marry rich, and you'll let your husband handle your son.

Sharon, you'd like to be counted among the number of ladies-who-lunch, but your tendency toward brashness excludes you from invitations to join their ranks. While the snub hurts you, you'll bounce back, creating your own organization of your select girlfriends, or you'll join an existing club that doesn't specify educational or financial requirements. These might include the Eastern Stars or the Continentals. Your hope is that your path will cross with the path of one of the social set's grand dames, and that this crossing will lead you into upper-class bliss. Here's a word to the wise, Sister Sharon: Don't count on it.

You see, Sharon, you, like Cheniqua, came up the hard way. You studied the outer trappings of success without internalizing the educational, financial, and social values

that come with it. This lack of observation and internal-
ization is the exact thing that keeps you running in place
on the treadmill of lower-middle-class existence. Sure,
you're doing better than most of your childhood friends
and maybe even some family members. Their standards
were much lower than the standards you selected, just as
your standards were lower than Cheniqua's. Nevertheless,
when you sit back in your black leather chair, you have to
admit that this is a long way from your humble begin-
nings.

Because you are simply searching for stability in your
life, you can find your Money Man just about anywhere,
though you'd prefer to meet him at an event like an
NAACP luncheon or a Masons' dance. (To you it sounds
more respectable than, "I met Tyrone at the bus stop.")
Because your Man Radar tends to point toward bum,
you've kissed quite a few frogs on your path toward finding your prince. The prince that you've found really tries
to do right by you à la Roc and Eleanor from the nineties
television show "Roc." No, he's not a screaming millionaire who is rolling in the dough, but he's all yours, and you
cherish him just as he cherishes you. In fact, Sharon, by
nature, your disposition is sweet, and that's why those
who know you, love you.

A woman I know, whom I'll call Shelly, is the epitome
of Sharon the Showgirl. Shelly, a matronly woman who
works as a teacher's assistant, came up the hard way. The
youngest girl in a large family, she inherited the looks that

had skipped over her older sisters. Shelly had been able to squeeze in two years of junior college before popping up pregnant by some local ne'er-do-well. Because of her devoted nature and her higher sights, she tried to stick things out with her son and daughter's father, but her efforts were to no avail. After they parted ways, Shelly returned to her mother's nest, kids in tow, intent on finding a way. She had brief gigs at dead-end jobs before landing at the post office, where she eyed her dreamboat. After a sweet courtship, Shelly and her construction worker beau tied the knot. Tired of the monotony of her job, she applied for a TA (Teacher's Assistant) job with a school district, and when she got it, she felt like she had hit the jackpot. Not only did she have summers off, but with that time came the opportunity to help raise her granddaughter, attempting to rewrite the families' song into one of uplift and prosperity.

While Sharon's brand of financial stability does not mesh with Simone's or Cheniqua's, it's enough for her. In comparison to where she began, she's come a long way, and no one can tell her that she hasn't. While she lacks the outward polish of Simone and the sensibility of Cheniqua, and while she'll drive people crazy with her mispronunciation of certain words (think et-e-qwette for etiquette), she'll demonstrate unparalleled devotion to family and close friends.

Sharon, by nature, is not observant. She's not refined enough to know that it's in poor taste to leave the price tag on a gift to show the recipient how much she paid for it, and with Sharon, pointing this out subtly will accomplish nothing. Reading is not high on her "to do" list, unless it's a book that has popped up as the popular must-read of the year. Sharon will find amusement at some of the traveling plays that are advertised on urban radio networks across the country. While Simone might find these plays to be completely classless, Sharon might see Cheniqua in the audience.

Other diversions Diva Sharon enjoys include, surprise, shopping. But she's not a bargain shopper like her aforementioned counterparts can be. Sharon goes for the gold because she feels like she deserves the best—best equaling most expensive, mind you—after all of her struggles and sacrifices. Her budget can afford her a few luxuries from "the right stores" if they're on sale, but she's not interested in just a few luxuries. This may be the only source of conflict between her and her Money Man. She'll try to convince him that she's not just buying for herself. "I'm buying for you, the kids, and the grandbaby, so you shouldn't complain," she'll say. In response, Sharon's Money Man will vacillate between two responses—either he'll try to convince her to curtail her spending some, or he'll pull overtime to appease his Glorious Diva. Whatever the outcome, Sharon's warmth and good heart will convince him that she's the only woman for him, so he should just save his complaints and be happy with his Diva.

SASHA THE SOCIALITE

Salary of potential Money Man	Millionaire
Career of potential Money Man	Self-made businessman (i.e., real estate developer, jeweler, restaurateur, transportation magnate)

Sasha, you play for keeps and you make no bones about it. You've been spotted tipping on daintily pedicured feet through chichi shopping districts such as Chicago's Magnificent Mile and its elite urban equivalents across the country and throughout the world. You wear your confidence, which can border on arrogance, like a badge of pride, and you silently command respect. If you must drive, only top-tier cars will do, and after you pull into the valet stand, you glide out of your elegant whip with all eyes on you. You truly are a princess, and you demand that people treat you like one. When you approach a door, and you happen to be weighed down, not only do people jump to open it for you, but they offer to carry your bags for you. You smile serenely and respond with grace, but in actuality, that is exactly what you were expecting.

Your palatial home is a blend of Cheniqua's chic and Simone's stylishness. You've commissioned artists to craft some original furniture pieces for you, and they've lived up to your expectations by selecting the most perfect wood they could find, and shaping it so that it would be fit for a queen. While many pieces are custom made, others are family heirlooms and fabulous finds from antique shops and flea markets. Flea markets? you ask. But of course, sugar. You know quite well that people overlook treasures that are right under their noses. (That's actually how you met your husband, but we're not ready to talk about that yet.) Baccarat, Swarovski, and Lalique rest comfortably around your castle, looking completely at ease next to monogrammed silver boxes you received for wedding presents. As for maintaining your palace, you don't lift a finger. Hazel comes in daily to attend to your domestic and culinary needs. You simply don't have the time to scrub and scour as your social calendar is packed. Even if it weren't, you find cleaning to be so, well, unappealing.

College was a finishing school for you, but you didn't view it as the thing to solidify your middle-upper-class status. You already knew who you were and where you were headed. You also recognized early that business runs America, so you didn't bother to pursue a graduate degree in some noble profession. You were more interested in returning to the real world rather than "A Different World." Education will, however, be important for your children, and you'll be a martinet when it comes to assuring that they are performing up to their intellectual abilities.

You and Money Man were thrilled with the arrival of your first baby, which came a few years into your marriage. As characteristic, you ignored familial protests to "get pregnant quickly," and you waited, thinking of the long-term implications of having children. Your children are spaced equally about two years apart, and with family honor and personal dignity in mind, they behave like angels. Exceptionally well rounded, your children are athletic and articulate, as they hold leadership positions on sports teams and academic clubs. They will rub shoulders with Simone's children in Jack and Jill, and your daughter will debut at one of the city's elite cotillions. Your children are as cultured as they are well rounded. After all, they've attended gallery openings and book signings with you ever since they could say, "Autograph, please."

As for your social obligations, Sasha, it's not terribly important for you to be the head honcho in your chapter's branch of the Links or the Junior League. You'll leave that to Simone, who gives good face. Instead, you'll work behind the scenes to stage some magnificent gala, and you'll accept with modesty the applause that you'll garner. In addition, you'll cochair a glamorous philanthropic event for the library or the museum just as easily as you'll participate in a walkathon to benefit breast cancer. You understand that you've been blessed, and you're willing to help those whose blessings aren't as visible.

Hobbies for Sasha can include playing mah-jong, attending fashion shows, traveling, and shopping. She's not reckless with money, though, which is a lesson that Sharon could stand to learn from her. She lunches often with other members of her circle or with those of the Simone class, but she's not big on treating. After all, she thinks, they can work as hard as I have and get the same results. This, by no means, says that she's not generous because she definitely is. She volunteers, gives to charities, sits on charitable boards in her community, and secretly pays the college tuition of some ambitious, intelligent relative. Yet she refuses to allow people to view her as an ATM.

Sasha's sense of style is strictly catwalk couture, but Sasha wanna-bes need not worry, for they, too, can afford many of the same pieces. She purchases from trunk shows and boutiques where she gets discounts because she's a good customer who knows that the ticket price in a boutique is just a suggestion. She also knows hole-in-the-wall spots that carry Christian Dior and a host of other top-notch designers. If she needs something special, Sasha knows at least one fashion guru who can design dynamic duds for her in no time.

Often, Sasha, you and your cohorts have middle-class roots. Though few would believe it, you're no stranger to hard work. They'd never imagine that you'd lift a finger on your precisely manicured (but acrylic-free) hands, but they couldn't be more wrong. It's your willingness to work that makes your husband adore you.

Your Money Man has not always had money. In fact, more often than not, he was as poor as the proverbial church mouse. He scrambled to get where he is, you know, negating naysayers and shattering stereotypes at every turn. His hunger for success is what drove him, just like tons of other paupers-turned-princes before him. (Think Ross Perot and A. G. Gaston.) In your youth, he was the slightly disheveled-looking guy whose ambition became manifest upon your probing journalistic questions. When you went off to college, he stayed on in your hometown, working tirelessly to save enough money and gain enough experience to open his own enterprise. Even if his first attempt failed, he learned from his mistakes, dusted himself off, and returned to the playing field. Meanwhile, from the sidelines, you cheered for him every step of the way. You saw the potential in him that no one else saw, and for that, he is indebted to you.

Your husband's business dealings have yielded tons of perks. Some of these include major discounts at high-end hotels, freebies at a variety of restaurants, free tickets to operas and concerts, and access to prime seats and boxes at athletic events. Your rolodex, which you guard ferociously, overflows with the personal lines and cell phone numbers of everyone from politicians to celebrities with roots in your city. Despite these ties, you maintain a measure of levelheadedness and are happy to have friends in all places.

Eileen lives the life of Sasha the Socialite, but no one would ever guess that it hasn't always been easy for her. Eileen and her husband, a prominent retailer, have been married for almost four decades. The two grew up in the same neighborhood, and they dated in their teens. Eileen was keenly aware of her future husband's sense of drive, and she also knew that he had a tough act to follow, as his own father owned a moving company as well as a supermarket. (Eileen's father-in-law did not believe in simply passing down wealth, especially to his sons, as he wanted them to come to the table with something they had brought on their own.) Upon marrying, the two purchased their own home, wasting no time with renting an apartment. Eileen's husband, who had done a stint in the Army, began working for a retailer, doing everything from keeping account of the stock to taking out the trash. Meanwhile, Eileen worked as a secretary for a religious organization. As they began to build a family, Eileen's husband began to build his plans for setting up shop. Finally, with nineteen years of experience and a wealth of wisdom under his belt, Eileen's husband walked away from his job to become his own man. He purchased a building in the business district of his city, and he rented the two floors above the store to a fashion designer. His wife worked side by side with him, doing accounting work, running errands, and being the softer female side to his harder edge. The fact that she was his accountant was a plus for Eileen because not only did her husband save money on those services, but she always knew exactly what was in the kitty. With a clientele that includes NFL and NBA athletes, newscasters, congressmen, and other high-profile people, Eileen is invited to so many events she can barely keep up. Her husband never forgot her devotion from the early days, so as soon as he was able, he showed his appreciation with a fur coat and a Mercedes. Now, several Mercedes and a Rolls later, Eileen is sitting pretty and sparkling all the way to the bank.

Sasha's Money Man treasures her immensely because she's supported him when he's experienced tragic lows and triumphant highs. Besides love, one of the reasons why her encouragement has been unwavering is because she recognizes that once a man has had money, he always knows how to make it again. Without complaint, she'll step in to do what needs to be done in order for the bills to be paid. In his business and social dealings, while other women may throw themselves at him, Sasha can still them with a glance. (Remember, she's not a porcelain doll; she has working- or middle-class roots, and while she's too refined to show them often, she will if she has to.) Her husband knows better than to even think about crossing her. He respects her too much, and he knows that since he is a self-made man without the benefit of a large inheritance and who had nothing before they married, things could get quite ugly, should a parting occur. He knows that it's cheaper to keep her. Besides, he adores her. Nasty thoughts aside, Sasha and her Money Man live a life that is enriched by their riches and their memories of obstacles overcome. Who says money can't buy happiness?

THINGS TO KNOW

Now that you've taken inventory and viewed your potential profile, there are a few things you need to know as you venture on your quest. These tips are all important, so consider them carefully because they could make all the difference in the world.

Thing 1: Go where the money is.

This tip seems obvious, but trust me, it's not. When you think of where money is, what comes to mind? Some Sharon types might think "casino" while some Cheniqua types might think "NBA play-offs." I want to invite you to open your minds to some other options. For example, several investment firms offer weekend breakfast seminars on financial planning. What better place to meet someone with a few nickels than at a seminar about how to increase your number of nickels?

Here's another example: In my business dealings, I've gone to sheriff sales to bid on properties. There are Money Men there who can fit just about anyone's criteria. There are attorneys there, representing families in peril. There are venture capitalists there, scouting out good properties to purchase, renovate, and sell. There are contractors there, advising venture capitalists of home rehab costs.

A graduate chapter of a notable sorority sponsored a charity event in which local male celebrities modeled and participated in a bachelor auction. These high-profile bachelors included a morning anchor for a news program on a local television station. Handsome and debonair, the anchor had been spotted around town with leggy women whose beauty trumped their intelligence. Despite his shallow choices in women, he was considered such a catch that he made one Glorious Diva lose all the cool points she had amassed through her professional dealings as a well-respected psychiatrist whose opinion is sought on local and national news shows. As Mr. Six-Figure Anchor strolled the catwalk, Dr. Diva reportedly threw her leg across the runway so he had no choice but to notice her. This began a high-profile courtship that was brilliant but brief. The diva was undaunted, though. Soon after, her social circle led her to an event where she met a media mogul who owned a cable company. They dated seriously, eventually becoming engaged, until he died suddenly of a heart attack.

Though she was undoubtedly heartbroken, especially when she stood at a flea market, peddling some of the possessions that he had amassed, you need not cry for her. As our brethren below the border say, "The South will rise again." This diva will throw herself back in the game, laying claim to another loaded loverboy.

One thing to keep in mind as you go where the money is, is that money knows money. One former Miss Virginia remembered that tip, and it made all the difference in the world for her. This James Madison University graduate married a comedian, actor, and millionaire extraordinaire in January 1995. Their marriage lasted just long enough to produce the couple's daughter before they parted ways about two years later. Did this glamorous doll mope around, wondering where her next Money Man would come from? Absolutely not. She was spotted and photographed at numerous events such as a wedding that appeared in *Jet* magazine. By staying active and on the scene, she cleverly remained visible. In 2000, the beauty queen adorned the arm of a popular football player, and they strode down the aisle in a lavish ceremony that reportedly cost $2,000,000. Their six hundred guests were serenaded by Kirk Franklin at their April 22 nuptials, which were performed by Bishop T. D. Jakes. Don't you just love to see us in prosperity? I sure do.

So again, I remind you to go where the money is, and you'll be in good company.

Thing 2: Money Men don't always look like Money Men.

Again, this sounds self-explanatory, but sometimes we need to reinforce some concepts. Simone might never entertain the thought of coupling with someone who doesn't wear a suit or at least a blazer to work. There's nothing wrong with wanting someone who looks refined and keeps his hands clean; however, in the process of trying to find Mr. Super-Clean and Paid, we might overlook Mr. Clean and Super-Paid. A potential Money Man might not always dress in the latest, most fashionable A-list duds, but he will make sure that his wife is well adorned.

In an old movie called *How to Marry a Millionaire,* actress Lauren Bacall portrays a model named Schatze, who, along with Betty Grable and Marilyn Monroe, is on a quest to lasso a lad who is rolling in the dough. She continuously rules one man out of her category of possibilities because he refuses to wear a tie, and by her standards, he is more than a little rough around the edges. Despite her attempts to clear her mind of all thoughts of him, Tom Brookman keeps resurfacing. Schatze passes up a chance to marry a clean-cut, obvious millionaire because, being honorable, she won't marry without love in the equation. (She's fallen for Brookman, who she believes is a gas station attendant, by this time.) It turns out that she gets what she wants because not only is Brookman worth more than the suave millionaire, but his list of assets is quite extensive. He owns commercial property in Manhattan, has livestock and oil concerns, and holds tons of stock. Schatze is able to have a "happily ever after" once she opens her eyes to all the possibilities.

Looking for a real-life example? Take millionaire Clark Howard. In countless interviews, the syndicated radio show host has boasted that he rarely buys anything new. He and his wife live in a seven-bedroom home in the metropolitan Atlanta area, but they furnished this sprawling elephant of a house with used furniture. Howard says that he grew up in a family that didn't practice financial savvy, splurging and living way above their means. When his father lost his job, the family hit a financial brick wall, and they all had to reevaluate their spending habits. When a $17,000 windfall befell young Clark, he simply invested it, and shortly after college he began a travel agency. His business grew so much that he sold it and was able to retire a millionaire before he hit thirty-one. The self-described tightwad refuses to spend $20 on a shirt, and his most lavish car is a new-model electric-powered Honda. He's so thrifty that he even purchased his wife's multiple-carat diamond ring from a warehouse-style discount store. Given all of this, you can be sure that Clark Howard is not "flossing" in the latest Versace threads, but he's probably got enough money to buy the company if he so chose.

In another example, my husband and I were at a real estate auction a few years ago. As I previously mentioned, there are Money Men of every description at these events; all a Glorious Diva needs to do is decide which type is right for her. Simone might be inclined to overlook someone like the contractor who was seated a few rows in front of us because, while buffed and handsome, he looked . . . well scruffy. He wore a navy blue T-shirt and matching baseball cap, dingy jeans, and construction boots. His chiseled arms were splattered with some kind of construction residue, and the hand towel hanging from his back pocket was the sure sign of a man who made his living by the sweat of his brow. This man, however, was all about business, and before the auction closed, he bid on and purchased three properties, totaling roughly $90,000. He had to leave a 10 percent deposit before leaving the auction, and he whipped out the $9,000 without breaking a sweat. And as he passed out of the room at the conclusion of his business, he walked with a cool, confident strut. While some like Simone, Cheniqua, and perhaps Sasha would judge this man from his attire and dismiss him as simply a common laborer, he was clearly situated well with regards to finances. That certainly reinforces the adage about not judging a book by its cover.

Now just as a Money Man might not always look the part, the converse is true as well. How many times have we seen a lot of flash only to realize that the "flasher" is just a fake? Just because a man, or any person for that matter, can blather on ad infinitum about how well off his friends are or drop some hush-hush hints about a deal he's working on, that doesn't mean he or she is holding. It could simply mean that the person is well read. As you set on your way, don't be fooled by outward appearances. And remember, in the words of Schatze, a real Money

Man never directly mentions his wealth. He merely refers to it by recounting some experience his wealth had afforded him.

Thing 3: Always look like a million.

Just because your Money Man might prefer a casual look while schlepping around, you can't afford not to look like a million bucks. Now don't misconstrue this to mean that you must always be dressed to the nines. Frankly, I find that to be a little restrictive for my day-to-day movement. However, you, Glorious Diva, should make it a point to look "fawine." Get a facial, manicure, and pedicure on the regular so that not only do you feel comfortable being pampered, but people get to see your pampered self as the norm. Even if you prefer the natural look à la Freddie from "A Different World," get those eyebrows arched and slather on some corn huskers before you slip into your Birkenstocks. And while fashion designer Carolina Herrera says that women over thirty should never leave the house without foundation, I'll make it a little simpler. Always wear mascara or eyeliner to open your eyes a bit, always keep your eyebrows arched, and always wear something on your lips, even if it is a tinted lip gloss.

Now, one simple but classic look that you can achieve on a modest budget is what I call Cambridge Cute. This look can be achieved by simply visiting the men's department of a Sears or JCPenney, and picking up some white, long-sleeved dress shirts. Then scoot over to the ladies department and select some form-skimming jeans. Swing by the costume jewelry department and scoop up an under-stated set of pearl earrings, a necklace, a bracelet, and a ring. A knock-off David Yurman set also looks great. As does a silver Stephanie (read Tiffany) jewelry ensemble. As for shoes and a bag, you might have to splurge on those because these are the markers of class. Or for a more creative option, you could go with a uniquely designed purse, which draws a little attention and says that you're not afraid to be different. (One of my favorite finds is a little lavender satin number with flowers embroidered on it. It was given to me stuffed with candy for a Valentine's gift. The sweets are long gone, but the bag is still adorable.) Stylish loafers in the fall and sleek mules in the spring and summer complement this look. And don't forget the sweater to drape over your shoulders. *Ça suffit!* That's it! In total, you might spend $200 for several sets of your Cambridge Cute uniform. The good thing is that the look is classic, so you won't have to worry about it going out of style.

Here's a bit of a reality check for us. The rich rarely buy retail. It's surprising, isn't it? Well, close your mouth for a second and think about it. Many of our country's rich are businesspeople, and being such, they recognize that products are marked up significantly before appearing on store shelves. Knowing that, they hardly ever cave in to the whims of purchasing straight from the shelves of high-end stores, unless they truly want to. You'll find more than a few millionaires, like Clark Howard, crowding into discount stores on the prowl for perfect purchases. In fact,

Eileen, a Sasha mentioned in the previous chapter, introduced yours truly to a number of discount stores in unseemly areas where Evan Picone and Christian Dior items were marked down to prices easily affordable by mere mortals like us. So, keep this in mind when suiting up to socialize.

Other simple but cute looks can be purchased at outlet malls, which usually have pared-down versions of high-end stores like Saks, Nordstrom, and Neiman Marcus, whose lower-end versions are Off Fifth, The Rack, and Last Call, respectively. The quality of the garments found here tends to be high, and the designers are easily recognizable, if that's important to you.

In addition to going with the Cambridge Cute look and shopping at the discounted high-end stores, Glorious Divas can achieve the million-dollar look by shopping at consignment stores in posh neighborhoods. One such store, Fashion Forward Designer Resale Boutique in Philadelphia's Chestnut Hill section, carries designers like Prada, Chanel, Hermès, Manolo Blahnik, and Gucci, among others. The proprietor, Ayana Mitchell, says, "My clients are very familiar with the type of designers that I carry, and they range from high school students to women over fifty." Mitchell says that by having consignors that are both in-state as well as in New York, Los Angeles, and Boca Raton, she is able to maintain a wide selection of cutting-edge, high-end couture pieces.

Finally, another option is to scour the racks at some "junk stores," you know, warehouse-like stores that sell fabric, summer wear, pillows, and arts and craft supplies. This is easy to do when you are a compact diva, size ten and under. Mama Rich, whose size ranges between a six and an eight, snags all kinds of delicious deals from stores that receive sample merchandise. Sometimes, the manufacturer might make a plug in the shoulder or shin of an ensemble to prevent a retailer from selling it, but if you're resourceful, you can patch the plug up easily with fusable webbing. You can also cover the slice in the shoulder with a scarf, a shoulder pin, or an exciting splash of a different fabric. You'll find that a ten-dollar Jones New York suit never looked so good.

Thing 4: Leave no stone unturned.

You've complained about them for years. The way some of them ogle at you and flirt innocently could turn you to putty or make you as mad as a wet hen. We've come to call them Dirty Old Men, but wait, could they simply be getting a bad rap?

Consider the case of a former *Playboy* Playmate of the Year. Born on November 28, 1967, this vivacious vixen had spent her early years in Mexia, Texas, and at the peak of her career there, she worked at a fast-food restaurant. In the early 1990s, she burst onto the fashion scene as the face of Georges Marciano's Guess? label. She was the flavor of the month for a Hollywood minute, but after a series of dead-end "B" movies and highly publicized antics, she spotted her Money Man. In 1994, the former model married an eighty-nine-year-old oil tycoon, and after a short married life together, he passed away leaving his estate in legal limbo, as his son battled the blond bombshell for a more sensible settlement. After a court case that seemed to last longer than the marriage, in February 2002, the former Playmate was awarded $88.5 million. Let me write that out for you: $88,500,000. At the risk of sounding crass, let me say, that's a hell of a lot of money.

Now, is it necessary to go to extremes and marry someone who is sixty-one years your senior for financial security? Not at all. Marriage is about companionship and communication. In my humble opinion, you might be able to relate better to someone who knows the difference between a television and a computer. So if he's a little older, perhaps a twenty-year span is sufficient.

Karen, a Colorado-based Glorious Diva who fits the Simone prototype, recently married an engineer nine years her senior. Their age gap is not a significant one; however, his age was enough to shore up his financial stability with the purchase of a home and other accoutrements that are characteristic of his status as a Money Man. Karen needed that brand of stability because she had not always made responsible choices or followed through with decisions that she had made (i.e., numerous transfers from college to college, multiple changes in career choices). Now, with the support of a mature Money Man, not only does Karen have an expensively decorated town house complete with Vera Wang stemware, Ralph Lauren sheets, and a Jacuzzi, but her husband has told her that she should stop working and go ahead to complete her graduate degree because his six-figure income will grant her that privilege.

What are the benefits of marrying a Mature Money Man? I'm glad you asked. For one thing, he'll be absolutely tickled that a pretty young thing is interested in him, and that is an ego stroker for sure. Besides, men love to feel superior, like they're introducing you to something new. If you are younger than your Money Man, chances are he'll get to fulfill his paternalistic wishes and get to flex his intellectual muscles.

Next, older men have had more years to work, accumulate wealth, and gain some measure of stability. Think about it. They are already established in their professions, and with the exception of the nasty downsizing trend that has swept the nation in recent years, they are well on their way to sitting pretty at the top of their games. They've had years of observation and grooming, and you, Glorious Diva, can slide right in without having to endure the struggle of the early years. Now mind you, in cases like this, you most definitely need to bring something to the table. If you are a writer, dazzle him with the various topics you've covered over the course of your career. If you are an educator, impress him with your passion for your students. Even if you are simply a showpiece, be the finest showpiece around with abs that he can bounce a quarter off of. Whatever your specialty, make sure that you're sizzling.

Besides the seasoned Money Man, you might also consider the widower. He's used to having someone around to complement him, so your chances of settling in might look pretty good. Be careful not to live in the shadow of the deceased because you'll always be the focus of comparison by him and others who knew them as a couple. Insist that you sell the old home and purchase a new one, and delicately suggest acquiring new furnishings and accessories to make the place really yours. Express sincerity as you propose giving some personal effects away to relatives and donating others to charitable organizations.

Admittedly, this option is a little more difficult because you might feel haunted by the deceased. Meals that you make never seem to taste quite right when compared to her version. A common fragrance that you coincidentally wear doesn't smell as sweet on you as it did on her. Tons of other comparisons made by your new husband (or his children—which is a matter we'll get to shortly) could threaten to drive you to a frantic frenzy; however, there is one thing that you must never do. Never demonstrate hostility toward the deceased because the dead can often evolve into angels in the eyes of the widowed. You'll look bitter and defensive if you say one cross word, so keep your lips shut. It's natural in just about all cases to feel a little jealous of someone whose been anywhere before you . . . including your lover's arms. But when you think about it, she's one of the reasons why he is the way he is. (Hopefully, this is a good thing.) She's warmed him up so that he now's trained and knows things that would have taken him years—your years—to learn. So in a way, you could thank her for breaking him in for you, instead of feeling overly anxious about your place in her shadow. Just keep in mind that your Money Man will recognize your worth as you set on your way down a new path together.

When children are involved, that opens up a whole new can of worms. The younger they are, the more pliant they are, and the more willing they are to give their stepmother a chance. Perhaps this stems from a need for maternal nurturing or a willingness to please the remaining parent. Whatever the rationale, it makes the situation easier to deal with. Things become a bit hairier when the children are older. In fact, sometimes, they can make things downright hard. What do I do, Ivana? I'm glad you asked. Stepparenting is never easy, and I'm not sure that anyone is equipped to respond to all of the possible things that can go wrong. Auntie Ivana has a few suggestions to help ease the transition.

First, be comforted by the knowledge that time heals all wounds. That means that patience is key. Just as it takes you time to warm up to a new person, it will take your stepchildren time. The first few months will be the most difficult, as you attempt to assimilate yourself into new surroundings and into their lives. Eventually, they will become accustomed to a new song being sung, new scents wafting up from the kitchen, and new ways of doing things.

Second, be yourself and try to form your own bonds with the children while being careful not to encroach too much upon their space. While you plan to be there for a while, you don't need to rush to form artificial bonds by insisting that they call you "Mom." You're not their mother, and don't expect to be accepted as such. The place that you hold, though, can and will be important, so respect that.

Third, develop original ideas for things you can do with your stepchildren. I stress original because you want to avoid any opportunity for them to say, "Mom never did it this way." In the process, the children will learn a little more about you, and they can come to see that you aren't the evil monster they envision stepmothers to be. You may even begin some new family traditions in the process. And who knows? They may end up developing new talents from something that you introduced them to.

Fourth, let the children see you and their father bond. Nothing solidifies the idea of the new marriage like seeing the two of you joined in marital bliss. Things will go much more smoothly if you maintain your composure and embrace your new role with dignity and grace.

Thing 5: If you don't marry him, you haven't caught him. He's caught you.

Vital lesson, ladies, so listen up. So many times, I've heard of women wasting critical years in relationships that turn out to be fruitless. In the end, they haven't gotten the man, the ring, or the desired lifestyle. A friend of Mama Rich's dated a man for almost fifteen years before realizing that he had no intentions of making an honest woman out of her. She had already purchased a wedding gown and for years had maintained the precise weight to fit into it, expecting to saunter down the aisle when the time came looking radiant and ravishing. An attractive, educated woman, she squandered her best years, keeping herself off the marriage market, for a dream. Words cannot convey the empathy and disappointment I felt upon seeing her wear the gown to a costume party after she kicked him to the curb when she realized that her dreams were dashed. In talking to her, I realized that she had worn the gown as an act of catharsis, yet I also read sadness in her eyes.

The lesson here? Gauge the landscape from the air before attempting to land. Note whether or not there are any obvious pitfalls. Scout the terrain closely to ascertain any hidden traps. Communicate with the target! There's no sense in trying to land if there are major obstacles in the way. The worst thing that could happen is thinking that you can make a safe landing, hopping out and getting stuck in a pit of quicksand, going nowhere. Not only have you wasted time, energy, and resources, but you've also completely trashed a fierce pair of Jimmy Choos!

Now, it would not have been necessary to say this years ago, but the second part of this lesson can save you grief, heartache, and shame. It's something that I've mentioned before, but it warrants repetition. Do not, I repeat, do not get pregnant by a potential Money Man with hopes of getting him to marry you. We've seen that show before, and the ending is almost always terrible. There are so many babies sprinkled across this country whose daddies are athletes and musicians, yet their lifestyles are none the better for it. Children are not pawns, and despite the advice given on a "how to trap a man" Web site, they should not be used as such, so don't even bring them into the picture. Aside from being cruel and ill thought out, it's rather low class and completely antithetical to what we're trying to do, which is elevate you to full diva status. And divas do not have "baby's daddies," they have husbands, so don't get caught out there.

Thing 6: Know how to keep your Money Man.

Philandering. Cheating. Stepping out. Creeping. Dipping out. Whatever you call it, it's infidelity, and some people believe that it comes with the territory when you're dealing in high stakes. Adultery is never par for the course, and the adulterer will have to answer for his or her actions at some point. In the meantime, I'll ask you, Glorious Diva, is that a price you're willing to pay in order to stay in the big game?

Jennifer swallowed down the pain of her Money Man's extramarital madness for years, but with each fling, he grew bolder and bolder until he decided that she was no longer worth the trouble. You see, Jennifer and her husband met while in college, and she was dazzled by his potential. Upon graduation, they married, and both of them began careers in education. Jennifer, an attractive petite woman, became pregnant, and her husband, seeking a more lucrative career for his burgeoning family, changed professions. As he traveled across the country, he learned that it was easy to "keep company" while on the road, so he had casual flings. As these flings grew to be normal, Jennifer looked the other way. Baby weight and loneliness expanded her hips, making her physically less appealing to her husband. Meanwhile, he developed an interest in business, so he went to Jennifer's mother for a loan to purchase a franchise of a major fast-food restaurant. Jennifer's mother consented, and Jennifer left her teaching job, replacing it with an apron as she prepared to work in the restaurant with her husband. One restaurant expanded into two, and their modest single-family home became a junior mansion complete with poolside sculptures. All looked well on the surface, but there was a crack in the interior. That crack came from a lack of respect in their marriage, specifically his disrespect of her. As cracks usually do, this one spread until it shattered the image, and after twenty-five years, two children, and countless affairs, Jennifer's marriage crumbled. She was reduced to moving into a two-bedroom apartment, and embarrassment temporarily forced her out of the social scene. She went back to teaching, enduring a humiliating pay cut and grasping at parts of memories of the past. In the years since then, however, she has reemerged from her cocoon, and like a true, resilient Butterfly Diva, she is glowing again.

How would you handle a situation like this? Realistically, you know that some women are like moths, and the brighter the shine, the finer they think your man is. Truthfully, you will have to prepare yourself for the onslaught of women who stealthily and boldly will come after your man. How will you handle it? That's the question. A Simone type is likely to break down and cry upon learning of any indiscretion on her husband's part, while Cheniqua might go after her husband with a knife. Sharon would be likely to threaten the woman, while Sasha wouldn't get mad at all. She'd get even by having a tryst on the side. It's a difficult dilemma, but you must decide how important your nuptial vows are to you. Can you deal with infidelity? If not, make it known from the door. That way you can avoid any confusion, should it arise.

Another point should be made, though some will call it an exercise in blaming the victim. While modern discourse spouted on talk shows points out that husbands don't cheat because another woman is prettier or sexier, I believe that in many cases, that's hooey. With that in mind, make sure that you keep yourself airtight from the beginning. It's an undeniable fact that childbirth changes most women's bodies. What do you do about it? You exercise throughout your pregnancy by going to the gym or even by taking long walks with your honey. This can serve as bonding time between you two, thus bringing you closer. After pregnancy, help your body to snap back in place with a girdle. (Some of us might need old-fashioned corsets to get that gut groovy again.) Maintain your outward appearance through aerobics and Pilates classes so that the adjustment from flab to fab can be made with ease. As for your inner beauty, childbirth does a lot to make mothers and fathers more reflective and peaceful, so suck it up. Bring in a nanny or an au pair to help you, also, so that when hubby comes home, you can be somewhat refreshed.

You must also consider intellectual stimulation for your sake and the sake of your marriage. Yes, by all means, bring hubby up to speed on baby's accomplishments, but know that endless prattle on baby's bowel movements can damper any dad's spirits. Read a book, take a class, or listen to NPR (National Public Radio). Anything to make yourself more well rounded and keep your husband's interest piqued.

Despite all that you do, however, there will still be some who will view your husband as their potential meal ticket. Remember Eileen? Well, she is constantly thrust into the position in which she must defend her territory. Because of her husband's business, he comes in contact with numerous potential customers, many of whom are female. Quite a few of them throw themselves at him despite the fact that they know he's unavailable. Always a respectful, respectable gentleman, he's learned to direct those types of customers to his wife, and she takes care of them. One day, one such pushy broad entered his establishment when his wife wasn't around. Their son was working that day, but the woman wouldn't even talk to him, as she insisted on being served by Eileen's husband. Wearing a very low cut blouse, the woman proceeded to lean over the counter pretending to inspect his wares while showing off her own. Eileen's husband very kindly asked her to leave after she "mistakenly" displayed an embarrassing amount of cleavage. He had made it clear that there was nothing she could do for him, but the woman was determined to get her claws on his money somehow. She returned to the store a few weeks later with her daughter, attempting to lure Eileen's married son to her side. Eileen happened to be present that day, and without missing a heartbeat, she invited the woman to leave and never come back. Eileen can anticipate being forced to defend her turf again, but she knows that it's worth defending. Besides, her husband is always a little friskier when she has flexed her muscles in that way.

PLACES
TO GO

Decisions, decisions. In your new life, you will have access to more disposable income. With more disposable income, you can have more fun. Think back to childhood. When you wanted to have fun, you went to the playground, right? Right. Like kids, adults in your new world have their own playgrounds. Following are some casual hideaways frequented by people in your new circle. This is, by no means, a complete list of vacations for the rich and famous. It is simply a guide to help you find fun places where you will be in like company. Let's take a look at some of these domestic spots and learn about some of the things to do there.

Oak Bluffs, Martha's Vineyard, Massachusetts

If you're into people watching and social climbing, you won't be disappointed. Visitors to the island have included former president Bill Clinton, attorney Vernon Jordan, politician Adam Clayton Powell Jr., and writer Dorothy West. There are numerous activities in which the magnetic mover and shaker can engage, and fortunately, most aren't limited to any specific time of year, although people are more apt to flock here in the spring and summer.

Things to do:

1. Lounge around the Ink Well, the beach whose name comes from the pigment of its regular inhabitants
2. Parties
3. Book signings and readings hosted by island residents
4. Shopping
5. Clambakes
6. Bridge games
7. Art lessons
8. Tennis tournaments

Glorious Divas who would be happiest here are Simone and Sasha, as they are both familiar and comfortable with the ways of the upper crust, who are regulars to this seven-square-mile village.

Sag Harbor, Long Island, New York

This retreat is home to many of black America's crème de la crème. Inhabitants include publisher and entrepreneur Earl Graves, American Express CEO Ken Chenault, and television host/former model/restaurateur Barbara Smith. Again, there are few set dates for the activities listed below, as they can be enjoyed anytime.

Things to do:

1. Parties
2. Sailing lessons
3. Art shows
4. Tennis
5. Annual Arts Festival (August)
6. Children's parade
7. Reading groups

Sasha and Simone would again feel most comfortable in this achievement-oriented group. Their accomplishments, financial standing, and experiences lend themselves well to the conversations that will take place.

Highland Beach, Maryland

This enclave has a wonderful history to embrace. Settled by the son of Frederick Douglass, it is situated about twenty miles southeast of Baltimore on the Chesapeake Bay. Famous visitors have included writer Paul Laurence

Dunbar and educator extraordinaire Booker T. Washington. Besides the Highland Beach Family and Friends Reunion, there are no set times to enjoy the following events.

Things to do:

1. Sailing
2. Visit Frederick Douglass's summer home and museum
3. Beach parties
4. Highland Beach Family and Friends Reunion (Labor Day Weekend)

Cheniqua and Sharon will feel right at home in these environs. Because of its proximity to Annapolis, Highland Beach might pique Cheniqua's curious nature and entice her to visit the historical sights so that she can impart lessons to her children.

Cape May, New Jersey

This southern New Jersey city is abuzz with activity from April through September. Not far from the City of Brotherly Love, Cape May is a site that is both serene and enchanting.

Things to do:

1. Cape May Jazz Festival (mid-April)
2. Secret Garden Tour (early May)
3. Gourmet Brunch Tour

4. Chef's Dine-Around (May)
5. Annual Cape May Music Festival (May-June)
6. Boardwalk Craft Show (June)

The activities and surroundings will appeal to Sharon, Simone, and Cheniqua. Sasha might find the events to be a bit too "down home," but she might enjoy downtime on the beach.

Idlewild, Michigan

This midwestern retreat saw its heyday in the early part of the twentieth century with visitors including Langston Hughes, Marcus Garvey, and Madame C. J. Walker. Though most of the glam is gone, it would still be a great place to visit for its historical value.

Things to do:

1. Horseback riding
2. Poetry in the Woods Festival (mid-June)
3. Parties
4. Annual Troutarama (July)
5. Mid-Michigan Idlewilders Annual Golf Tournament (mid-July)

Simone and Cheniqua might appreciate spending some time here, but Sasha and Sharon might find it a bit drab for their tastes.

Myrtle Beach, South Carolina

This South Carolina hot spot has gained popularity over the years, and the high-rise hotels are proof of this. Nightclubs and restaurants punctuate just about every block, and you never know whom you'll run into on the links.

Things to do:

1. Camping
2. Annual Birding Festival (February)
3. Golf
4. Water sports (i.e., deep sea fishing, cruising the water-ways)
5. Annual Good Time Car Show
6. Lounging on the beach

There is something for every Glorious Diva at this hot spot. There are malls and water parks in the area, and the car show and golf courses will definitely be a hit with the Money Men. Consider this for family vacations.

Hilton Head, South Carolina

This twelve-mile island along the East Coast is a fun getaway for families, couples, and singles alike.

Things to do:

1. Lounging in the sun
2. Golf

3. Tennis
4. Art galleries
5. Christmas Count Prep (sponsored by Audubon Society)
6. Bicycling
7. Boating tours
8. Fishing
9. Shopping

Like Myrtle Beach, Hilton Head has something for every Glorious Diva and her family. Housing developments are springing up all over the place, and many older divas are retiring to this enticing island.

Savannah, Georgia

This Southern city has a rich history and an exciting future. Credited as Georgia's first city, Gullah traditions remain alive in the city today because of its closeness to the sea. The city is renowned for its beauty, and legend has it that General Sherman presented the city as a Christmas gift to President Lincoln in December 1864. Despite its tumultuous, slavery-marred past, Savannah is a city that enjoys Southern gentility and metropolitan charm.

Things to do:

1. International dining experiences
2. Haunted History Tours
3. Museums (i.e., Mark Gilbert Civil Rights Museum and Telfair Museum of Art)

4. Shopping on River Street
5. Antiquing

Simone, Sasha, and Cheniqua will enjoy this city with its comfortable formality and relaxed elegance. Sasha and Simone will be enchanted by the mansions on the former plantations, while Cheniqua will dive into the contemporary pleasures that the city offers. It might be a bit too "mossy" and laid back for Sharon's taste.

Atlanta, Georgia

This bustling Southern city is becoming known as a magnet for Glorious Divas in the South. With former mayors like Andrew Young, Bill Campbell, and Maynard Jackson, the city is filled with "people in brown putting their things down." With restaurants popping up all over, and luxurious malls to suit any budget, Atlanta represents the face of the new South with prosperity in full bloom.
Things to do:

1. National Black Arts Festival (mid-July; visit www. nbaf.org for more information)
2. Film Festival (mid-June)
3. Annual Yellow Daisy Festival (early September)
4. Crepe Myrtle Festival (early August)
5. Alpharetta's Main Street Market (visit www. alpharetta.ga.us)

6. American Indian Festival (May & October)
7. African American Panoramic Experience (changing exhibits)
8. Atlanta History Center (visit www.atlantahistory center.com)
9. Golfing
10. Shopping

Every Glorious Diva will love this rich city. Large enough to be called "The New Black Mecca" yet small enough to still have quaint sections, Atlanta is a Southern jewel. Affluence abounds as much as Southern hospitality, and everyone can find his or her niche.

Rehoboth Beach, Delaware

This tiny beach south of Dover is a delightful setting for fun in the sun and romance. A haven for high-powered Philadelphians, Rehoboth Beach offers charm and class for its visitors.

Things to do:

1. Rehoboth Beach Autumn Jazz Festival (mid-October)
2. Sea Witch Halloween Festival (late October)
3. Rehoboth Beach Film Festival (early November)
4. Water sports
5. Fine dining

6. Dancing
7. Fishing and crabbing
8. Day spas
9. Golfing
10. Shopping
11. Camping

This is the perfect hideaway for Simone and Sasha, as they will be in their element rubbing shoulders with the visitors who frequent this East Coast sanctuary.

South Beach, Florida

This newly revived section of Miami received a shot in the arm in the early eighties when investors saw opportunities for revitalization, and they swooped in. With attractions like the Miami Beach Art Deco District, which is on the National Register of Historic Places, plenty of high-end Hollywood types have been spotted in this twenty-four-hour-a-day playground. They include Sylvester Stallone, Calvin Klein, Madonna, and Robert DeNiro, so if you're into people watching, this is definitely your place.
Things to do:

1. Dancing
2. Swimming
3. Fine dining
4. Shopping

5. Walking tour
6. Bicycling
7. Rollerblading
8. Visiting museums (i.e., the Bass Museum and the Wolfsonian Museum)

This is the Diva's Den for Sharon, Sasha, and Cheniqua because of its exciting nightlife and "Miami Vice"-esque scenery. Great eats and eclectic cultural experiences are promised. This scene might prove to be a bit too flashy for Simone's taste, but she'll live vicariously through the pictures you share.

West Palm Beach, Florida

This Florida jewel is considered one of the most relaxing realms of the region. With forty-seven miles of beaches and weather that is consistently agreeable, West Palm Beach should rank high on your list of vacation vistas.
Things to do:

1. Golfing
2. Playing tennis
3. Visiting the International Orchid Center
4. Canoeing on the Loxahatchee River
5. Checking out the Clematis by Night Fountain Side Concert Series
6. Shopping on Antique Row

7. Visiting Lion Country Safari
8. Fine dining

There is something to do for all of the divas in this lo-
cale, so add it to your "places to go" list.

Other Hot Spots

There are plenty of other great places domestic and abroad
to go in your new life. Different divas enjoy different activities, and because of their diverse tastes, I have divided
sample activities among the prospective divas. Remember,
there may be overlap, but that simply means that there are
more places for you, Glorious Diva, to explore.

Simone

Simone is likely to enjoy activities like skiing, sunning,
and shopping as forms of relaxation while on vacation. So,
Simone, honey, tap that Money Man of yours on the
shoulder and point him to the places you'd like to go.

For skiing, you might drop in to the Poconos in Pennsylvania. This mountainous region sits on the borders of
New York, New Jersey, and Pennsylvania, and it promises
plenty of pleasure at some of the romantic hideaways.
Simone, you might also try the Swiss Alps as another skiing spot. Switzerland, once known for having little to no

nightlife, has revitalized itself to improve tourism. You're always one for cultural enrichment, so after you get the kids to bone up on their French, book your flight and come on over.

For fun in the sun, Simone, you might venture to the British and U.S. Virgin Islands. Another hot spot that has made its way onto the map for chic travelers is the Dominican Republic. People are raving about Punta Cana, and it definitely is worth the exploration, as is Curacao, one of the ABC islands (Aruba and Bonaire being the other two). Situated close to South America, Curacao is outside of the storm belt, and it enjoys tropical breezes and temperatures that max out in the mid-eighties. The islanders will greet you in English, so don't worry about language barriers. Just come on down because the water is fine.

As for shopping, Simone, you can pick up cultural items you adore from Morocco, known for its colorful tiles and housewares, and Ghana, known for its beautiful textiles. These places will not only provide you with great items to incorporate into your home, but also enlighten you and yours about the place where mankind was born. Finally, what is springtime without Paris? Aside from promising heady romance for you and your Money Man, you can cruise the flea markets for cool finds and explore the lingerie shops for hot pieces. (It's no wonder that well-to-do Cubans have sent their engaged daughters over there for decades in search of fantastic foundations.)

Cheniqua

Cheniqua, in general, you're not one for too much time in the cold, so you're inclined to pass on skiing. Instead, you might enjoy watching others take their chances with Lady Luck. You might be convinced to try your hand, but practicality and parsimony prevail, dictating that you venture no further than the slot machines. Places where you're apt to be found gambling include Paradise Island in the Bahamas, where you'll also frolic in the water, careful not to mess up your new "do." Las Vegas might also lure you in, and you'll definitely enjoy the sights in Sin City, but you'll remind your Money Man not to look too hard at the . . . ahem . . . sights.

Sunny spots that pique your interest include Saint Thomas and Barbados. You might also be drawn to Jamaica because of the phenomenal food and the beauty of places like Ocho Rios. In Jamaica, you're likely to run into Sharon, who, with her love for bright colors and lively surroundings, will fit right in.

Although you love fashion, you're not inclined to be adventurous in your shopping exploits. You figure, why spend money to spend money, so you're likely to shop stateside. Your love for leather might, however, lure you to Italy, where you'll meander through Milan and roam around Rome on a quest to verify the existence of the houses of Fendi and Gucci. Then, you and your husband will trot back home with gifts for everyone because you're just a generous kind of gal.

Sharon

Sharon, you approach the idea of vacation with vivaciousness, but rather than explore and learn on your trips, you just want to have fun. And there's nothing wrong with that.

The places where you're likely to go for gambling are primarily stateside, and that's fine for you. Foxwood, Connecticut, suits your fancy, and you might be inclined to visit some of the shops displaying Native American wares, specifically the jewelry. You'll purchase some silver pieces that you'll wear with pride, tempted to represent them as platinum to the ignorant. For gambling, you might also enjoy *la vida* in Las Vegas because of its brilliance. You'll tire out your Money Man with your immersion in the activities, but you won't fret. You'll simply kiss him and tell him that you'll catch him on the rebound before sending him off to the hotel room.

As for lying out in the sun, you're not that adventurous, opting for places where you can pick up a hint of color to impress your friends. They can't be too far, though. Your favorite sun spot is Jamaica, but you're not opposed to bopping down to the Bahamas.

Sasha

Sasha, Sasha, Sasha. In the words of writer and anthropologist Zora Neale Hurston, you do not weep at the world, for you are too busy sharpening your oyster knife. The world is yours, and nothing will stop you from traveling around it to find your pearl.

The first stop on your shopping trip is Aruba, where you'll find emeralds galore. You're also open to some European spots like Poland, renowned for its stores of amber, and Prague, which has great everything, including crystal. The lingerie shops and boutiques of Paris also capture your fancy.

As for sunning, you won't be limited by geographical boundaries, and you're willing to go just about anywhere. After all, the world is yours, and your first stop is Greece. You and your family will explore the thousand islands and be captivated by sites like the Parthenon and the ancient castles. Another sun-drenched site you'll enjoy is Grand Cayman among the Cayman Islands. Known for being the stomping ground for countless celebs, you'll don your shades and roll with the rest of them, taking in the beauty of the beaches.

Gambling locations that might attract your fancy include San Juan, Puerto Rico, where you'll salsa with the natives between spins of the roulette wheel. Monaco, a traditional playground for the rich, is another venue that you might visit. While there, you'll browse in the boutiques catering to the affluent and you'll also catch some sun.

On the opposite end of the weather spectrum, you might bump into Simone while skiing on the Swiss Alps. Stateside, you're apt to go to Colorado, where Vail and Aspen beckon to you. Whether you cruise the mountains or stay by the fireplace in the lodge, you'll have a blast.

ACTING
JUST SO

We all know that money does not necessarily equal refinement and class. There are plenty of people who don't have much in the way of worldly possessions, yet their hearts are gold, as evidenced by their thoughtful gestures, generous giving, and kind deeds. There are others whose bank accounts are in overdrive, yet they are at a loss as to how to behave in proper society. Some of us call it poor manners, while others of us call it acting "project-ish." Whatever the name, it will never do, so let's get a few things in order, shall we?

Before we do, let me share with you an anecdote illustrating my point. In my work, I've had the privilege of traveling to many regions of the country, and by far I can say that the ladies of the South, specifically Georgia, have us all beat when it comes to gentility. They have raised the art of being cordial to a whole new level. Once while visiting a Glorious Diva from Atlanta, we had to make a road trip to Augusta to take care of a few things. Before getting on the road, we stopped to fuel up her Mercedes. My city instincts sent me rushing around the gas station and the convenience store, grabbing goodies to grub on so that we wouldn't have to stop while on the road. She strolled leisurely along, holding a conversation with the attendant, debating on whether or not to get hot tea or coffee, going to the ladies' room to adjust her hair and freshen her makeup, and just chilling. While observing her, I suddenly figured out why it took so long to fight the Civil War. Now, mind you, once she got behind the wheel, she floored it, and we got to Augusta with enough spare time to head to the ladies' room to check our appearance.

Southerners, like the French, will stand on ceremony and work at their own pace, regardless of their surroundings and the schedules of others. Even Southerners who don't have a lot of money will take time to welcome visitors with food or at least a glass of lemonade. Like old Wilford Brimley says, "It's just the right thing to do."

What follows is by no means a comprehensive "how-to" in home training, but it is, quite simply, a miniguide for putting your best foot forward. Although we've lost a great deal of the formality that governed our lives in the past, it is nice to observe and revive some traditions. It brings order to our lives, and it simply makes us appreciate the pleasantries of life. Being well versed in etiquette does not have to mean being able to discern Wedgewood from Mikasa from a mile away. It simply means presenting the best image of yourself that you can possibly show.

Before we begin, you must know that the governing rule to acting "just so" is to demonstrate grace. What is grace? you ask. (I'm so good that I should be a mind reader.) Well, it is defined in many different ways. Synonyms for grace include *elegance, refinement, polish, beauty, poise, charm,* and *style.* Because those nouns are intangible, allow me to point out some women whose actions exemplify grace.

Think Marian Anderson. Now, remember that ugly spectacle from 1939 when she was slated to sing at Constitution Hall in Washington, D.C., but her performance was banned by the Daughters of the American Revolution. Rather than poke her lip out and pout like a child, and rather than open a can of Philly whoop-ass on them, Lady Anderson stuck out her chest, clasped her hands before her diaphragm, and sang on the steps of the Lincoln Memorial to the 75,000 listeners who had gathered to hear her mellifluous contralto voice. That's grace.

Think Josephine Premice. The Haitian-American entertainer oozed elegance and reeked of regality. Nominated for Tony Awards, this woman experienced her share of the harsh racial realities of her day, but she never lowered her standards or bowed her head under the pressure. Her daughter, television and film director Susan Fales-Hill, remembers her mother's admonition about keeping good face even under adversity. In an article that appeared in the

December 2001 issue of *Town & Country*, Fales-Hill shared her mother's "first commandment" of diva training: "Smile, dress well, and apply copious mascara though your heart is aching." According to Fales-Hill, Premice internalized her own advice, getting completely decked out in an outfit complete with ruby slippers four months before her death although emphysema wracked her body. That's grace.

Think Jacqueline Kennedy Onassis. Known as one of the most photographed women of the century, Mrs. Onassis suffered a loss up close that most of us could only feel from afar. Despite losing two babies, despite rumors of her husband's infidelity, despite witnessing her husband's murder, and despite the probing public eyes, her shoulders remained set squarely as she moved from the White House to a life outside the political circle. That's grace.

Is it necessary to have endured loss in order to possess grace? Absolutely not. One must have grace to endure the loss with dignity. Trying times impel grace to come forward, but it most certainly emerges from within. Grace is the thing that keeps us from gloating when we've advised someone and they've chosen another way, only to learn that our way was the right one. Grace is the thing that keeps us from getting "cocky" when it looks as if the world sits in our laps. Grace is the thing that keeps us from "showing out" when we have every reason to do so. Now mind you, it doesn't mean being a pushover, but it's allowing your silent actions to speak for themselves.

Some other tips to consider when considering grace are as follows:

1. Don't beg the question.

This is a major pet peeve. If you have something to say, just say it. Don't hint around at something, hoping that the listener will ask you the desired question. Not only is it annoying and immature to drip a little of what you want known in the conversation, but it makes you look desperate. If you want to create an air of mystery, there's a smoother way to do it.

2. Keep in touch.

We are all so busy these days that we can barely make time for ourselves, let alone anyone else. And it seems that the more we move forward technologically, the less in touch we are. Even if we don't have time to chatter on the phone for hours, it's always nice to know when others are thinking about us. Most of us are thrilled to receive anything in the mail besides bills. We all appreciate a handwritten letter every now and then, so why not give what we like to get? Before you do, be sure to pick up some stylish stationery.

3. Banish your cell phone.

We have all borne witness to the serene setting that was interrupted by the obscenely piercing ring of a cell phone. While some of us need them for business, and others need them for family emergencies, some people use them as accessories, neglecting etiquette edicts against blabbing in public places. Again, cell phone chatterers run the risk of appearing too desperate for attention as well as annoying others when they can't resist the urge to converse.

4. Monitor your speech.

Aside from being offensive to others, boisterous banter also makes chatterers look bad. Many dinners have been ruined by diners at the next table who can't control their conversation level. Some people think that they will look important if they name drop and others overhear the content of their conversations. In addition to the tone of the conversation, no one should ever hear you use profanity in public. It's just so . . . common.

5. Don't strive to be the center of attention.

We all know people who not only monopolize conversations, but also happen to know a little something about every topic of conversation that arises. Or we know of celebrities whose outrageous antics keep them in the public eye. This type of display smacks of insecurity, perhaps stemming from being overlooked in earlier years. Whatever the cause, it's bad form. When we are truly dynamic and dynamite, people will notice us. Besides, most people appreciate folks who are good listeners much more than those whose constant blathering interrupts good solid discourse.

With these basic tips in mind, we are on our way toward Graceland, but don't pack just yet. There are a few other things you need to know.

Grace is evident from our carriage. Aside from the health benefits of maintaining good posture, the way in which we carry ourselves dictates the way we feel about ourselves. It is my personal belief that every little girl should take at least five years of dance training, beginning with ballet classes. The poise with which a young girl learns to carry herself shapes the way others perceive her. With shoulders back, necks elongated, rib cage elevated, and stomachs held in tightly, we look royal, and as I said before, when we look royal, people are more inclined to treat us royally.

Achieving true grace takes quite a few years of cultivation, so if you don't have it already, don't expect to get it immediately. Start by practicing the art of restraint. That means pause before you say the first thing that pops into your head. By doing so, you give yourself some thinking time, you might save yourself some embarrassment, and you'll definitely come across cooler and more relaxed. In addition, restrain yourself when it comes to eating, and restrain yourself when it comes to acting on your impulses.

It's About Time

Speaking from personal experience, I will tell you that it's not a good thing when people undervalue my time.

From healthcare practitioners to hairstylists, I detest slow people. After a bout with an unpleasant rash, I found myself in the waiting room of a prominent dermatologist. He came highly recommended by my primary-care physician as well as good friends, so I figured that I could expect a fifteen-minute wait. When fifteen minutes turned into a half hour, I turned to another patient to ask if this type of wait was normal. She said casually, "Oh, yeah, girl. I've never been seen within the hour of my appointment."

You can imagine that my jaw dropped. I was vulnerable because my skin condition needed treatment, yet my dignity demanded that I be seen soon. Armed with a magazine and the ability to curse in French, I stewed silently in the waiting room for another forty-five minutes. When I was finally seen, steam was rising from my ears. Before I let him diagnose and treat my condition, I cleared my throat and checked my watch noticeably. (Remember, Glorious Divas never show out in public.) I didn't have to say a word because his apologies began flowing profusely. Always gracious but not to be played with, I politely informed him of my expectations and asked him if he was willing to comply. He agreed, and that was that. I've returned to the office a few times, but I have never had to endure the wait again.

The lesson here? There is nothing more frustrating than having all of your ducks in a row and ready to go, and someone else is slow. We've all been on the receiving end of the chronologically challenged, so we know that it's bad form to dish it out. If you happen to be running late for an appointment, by all means, call. If it looks as if you won't be there within fifteen minutes or so, reschedule. It's more considerate than expecting others to wait and conform to your schedule.

What's Mine Is Mine; What's Yours Is Mine

When friends borrow, it's best that you let them know your needs up front. If you need the tool back before next weekend, make sure that they know so that no one's feelings get hurt.

There are some people we know who are bad borrowers. To avoid any confusion, say no if you believe that borrowing this item is problematic. Explain your side, but don't be swayed from your initial decision. If you are feeling generous, buy one for the person as a gift.

If you are the borrower, you must remember to return the item in a timely manner and in the same (if not better) condition than when you borrowed it. It's actually one of the laws of the universe that help to keep the environment from being in a state of decline. Why not employ the same idea when it comes to something you borrow? If the object in question is a friend's blazer, make sure that no buttons are loose and take it to the dry cleaner before bringing it back. If it's a necklace, polish it before returning it. These things take very little effort, money, or time, and practicing them keeps a friendship running smoothly.

Telephone Etiquette

It should go without saying that the telephone should always be answered in a dignified, courteous manner, but sometimes people, especially teens, need a little reminding. Some appropriate ways to answer the telephone include: "Good afternoon, Smith residence," "Smith residence," "Good afternoon," or simply "Hello."

When leaving a message on an answering machine, speak slowly and clearly, and leave a number where you can be reached. Don't be too long-winded because the answering machine might limit the recording time. When leaving a message with a teen, spell your name for him or her. If the young person isn't prepared to take a message, this signals that he or she should.

When a message is left for you, be prompt in returning it. When possible, abide by the twenty-four-hour return call rule.

Mi Casa Es Su Casa

When you're the guest . . .

It's a blessing to have friends and family who open their homes to us, and we should count it as such. To help keep friendly relations flowing freely, I offer these simple tips.

1. Don't overstay your welcome.

Although your host may insist that you stay as long as you wish, use common sense. If he or she has been awake since the wee hours of the morning preparing for the bash, it's rather rude for you to close the house down, unless this is a very good friend who likes to recap with you after an event.

2. Sincerely offer your help.

Ask what you can do to ease the strain of hosting a party or a weekend stay. If the host says he or she needs no help, avoid being underfoot.

3. Bring a hostess gift.

Instead of being a chore, this activity can be fun. Aside from the usual candle/bath kit that many people give, you can give a theme gift. If you're invited to a garden party, arrive with a plant arranged in an upside-down hat that acts as a planter. If you're invited to a friend's cabin in the woods, bring a basket containing marshmallows, roasting twigs, hot chocolate, mugs, and cookies.

4. Leave things in the same condition in which you found them.

Show respect and appreciation by cleaning up after yourself. If you mistakenly break or damage something, don't try to hide it. Tell the host/hostess immediately (not once you are in the safety of your own home), and make a genuine offer to pay for it. If it's something that you can replace on your own, save your friend the trouble of going to the store by doing it yourself.

Another thing that shouldn't require mentioning is the RSVP. The phrase is French, and it's an acronym for *"Répondez s'il vous plaît."* In English that's simply "Respond, please." A friend of mine, frustrated with the lack of consideration granted by invitees to her many shindigs, included the following humorous line under RSVP: "Dat mean, call to let me know if you comin'." Hosts and hostesses spend a lot of effort preparing food (or paying for it to be catered) and arranging seating. It's downright disrespectful and rude not to reply. If the invitation reads, "RSVP Regrets Only," that means call if you're not coming. It's something that's very simple, but when it's done, it can spare hurt feelings and save loads of time.

When You're the Host . . .

Event hosting is so much easier when you've done the planning far in advance and started the work in enough time to ensure a smooth affair. Keep these things in mind as you plan for your big shindig:

1. Check food preferences before the event.

Because of religious restrictions, allergies, and dietary needs, there are certain dishes that some people cannot eat. This does not have to throw a wet blanket on your event. If you're having a small affair like a dinner party, you really should check with your guests about culinary preferences. This will avoid hurt feelings and wasted energy on the actual day of the event. For a larger event, have a variety of foods so that there is something for everyone.

2. Set boundaries.

If you prefer that people not smoke in your home, do not have ashtrays around. If someone lights up anyway, quietly ask him or her to go outside to smoke. If you find that some guests are doing something that you find objectionable in your home, ask them to refrain from such behavior or ask them to leave. There is no shame in protecting your home environment. After all, your home is your castle.

3. Create a comfortable environment.

If you have guests staying over, leave toiletries and refreshments where they have easy access to them. Anticipate needs to avoid discomfort in asking for things.

4. Give kids their space.

Parents should keep in mind that not everyone is as tolerant of other people's children as they are of their own, so your own children should be well behaved. If your friends have children and you don't, there are a lot of things that you need to consider when hosting an event. First, have a safe, spare room for the kids to play and interact in. Second, consider hiring a respectable teen from your church or neighborhood to "hold down the fort" in the area where the kids will be. Third, have an ample supply of "kid things" like videotapes, toys, and games around to amuse them. Next, have kid-friendly foods like hot dogs, sandwiches, and French fries for them to munch on, as they might consider your bleu cheese and crab fajitas a bit much for them to consume. Finally, have parents check in on them periodically to ensure that things are running smoothly. As the hostess, you might peek in a time or two as well, just to make sure that the sitter doesn't need reinforcements and to make sure that the children's room is under control. Children are more likely to behave if an adult will be unexpectedly popping in to check on them.

Party Ideas

Entertaining is one of the highlights of the high life. Party planning gives some people anxiety, while others look for excuses to roll out the red carpet. Whatever your mind-set, throwing a bash can be super fun if you have a plan. If you don't, hire a party planner who can handle the tough stuff for you.

Below are some party ideas and ways to implement them:

1. Themed Super Bowl parties
The 2002 Super Bowl was held in New Orleans, and party ideas were abundant, seeing that New Orleans natives are known for their healthy attitudes about letting their hair down. I attended one well-thought-out party, and despite the fact that I don't know a defensive end from a tight end, I had a great time.

My host greeted everyone with Mardi Gras beads in a basket. In addition, Mardi Gras beads adorned the African statues gracing their chic home. New Orleans–style jazz played on the first floor of their spacious palace, getting guests in a festive mood, and football decorations sat in key locations throughout the house. Football festivities were focused primarily in the basement, but guests were free to settle in the quieter parts of the house. Food included Cajun-style cuisine such as gumbo and crayfish cakes paired with traditional game day snacks such as wings and hoagies. Kegs of beer and wine sat in a weight room/bar area, where they were easily accessible to party-goers.

The party was a blast. I learned a lot about New Orleans. I still don't know a thing about football.

2. Decade parties

These events are always fun, as they allow guests to reminisce about times past. Don't be content simply to play music from that era, though. Insist that your guests sport the hairstyles and be garbed in the attire of that day! For a seventies party, scatter appropriate board games around, and partygoers will revel in their opportunity to play Connect Four once again. Playing Twister might prove to be a little more complicated with all of the old bones around, but the plastic game board will serve as a wonderful area rug. Scour thrift stores for knickknacks from the time period, and place them strategically throughout. If you have any old posters from popular television shows, stick them up as well. You'll get a kick out of remembering how much you loved Ponch from "CHiPs."

3. Juneteenth celebrations

Aside from the historical and cultural significance, these bashes can serve as reunion events. A Juneteenth cookout that yours truly planned consisted of games that gauged the cultural knowledge of youngsters (i.e., black facts flash cards), music reminiscent of the civil rights struggle (i.e., Sam Cooke's "Change Gon' Come"), and gourmet twists on foods that have meant a lot to us (i.e., fried grits with a seafood sauce). The theme souvenirs for the event were gift bags containing an authentic stalk of cotton and a minibottle of wine with a personalized message reading, "In remembrance of our past and in celebration of our future." Having a minister from your local church say grace and invoke remembrance would be a wonderful addition to a Juneteenth celebration as well.

4. Lovers' lunch

A good time to plan this couples-only event is around Valentine's Day. Elements include foods that inspire aphrodisiacal delight such as champagne and strawberries, smoked oysters, and crème brûlée in heart-shaped flan dishes. (Don't worry. You can pick them up at Crate & Barrel.) Each couple is required to bring a love poem to be read during lunch and a love ballad to add to the ambiance. Plan for the event to last for two to three hours, so that the evening can be free for . . . other things.

An alternative could be a "Sweaters and Sweeties" event planned around the Christmas and Kwanzaa holidays. All guests must wear sweaters and they must bring dessert.

5. Kids art show

In the spirit of creating community, this event will validate your children by showing appreciation for their efforts. Just like an adult art show, the children's work should be framed and placed on easels with the names of the artists prominently displayed in a lower corner of the picture. Discourage parents from bidding solely on their children's work by having each student give a minipresentation on their work, the materials used, and the meaning of the picture. The proceeds can go either to a scholarship fund, to the local children's hospital, or to a charity that benefits kids. Allow the children to be present to make the presentation to the charity.

6. Mother-daughter tea

This event is best saved for the time near Mother's Day; however, any time is a good time to celebrate the special bond shared by mothers and daughters. As is customary for a tea, light fare should be served. Again poetry and songs celebrating motherhood are encouraged. An additional requirement could be for each participant to share a story that epitomizes her admiration for her relative. Have plenty of tissues on hand, as you can expect tears to be flowing by the end of the testimonials.

When we think of light fare for such an event, we think

of hors d'oeuvres and light salads. The hors d'oeuvres can be hot or cold, although as hostess, you might save yourself some wear and tear if you keep the event indoors, where you have easy access to the oven for warming hot hors d'oeuvres or the fridge for chilling cold ones.

I'm feeling a little generous, so I'm going to share something with you: my top ten favorite hors d'oeuvres for such an event! These selections, while they look complicated, are quite simple, and trust me—they are definitely crowd pleasers. You can cheat with some of them, like the Mini-crabcakes (Phillips brand are delicious), the Miniquiches, and the Fresh Fruit and Cheese Tray, by purchasing them at the store. The others are simple and take minimal time. Take a look.

a. Spinach and Parmesan Wontons

Mix a bag of fresh spinach with two tablespoons of Parmesan cheese and two tablespoons of mayo. Stir in a little seasoned salt. Take wonton wrappers and fill them with the spinach mixture. Lightly panfry, let cool a bit, and serve.

b. Chicken Skewers with Mango and Brandy Sauce

Skewer seasoned boneless, skinless chicken breasts and bake until done. Using a blender, mix mango pulp, raisins, sugar, and a touch of brandy. After tasting, warm the sauce and serve.

c. Salmon and Cream Cheese on Heavy Crackers

While baking thinly sliced pieces of salmon, spread

cream cheese on heavy crackers. Dress the crackers with the cooked salmon and add capers for garnish.

d. Shrimp and Feta Filo Cups

Season and steam shrimp before filling filo cups with them and feta cheese. Bake until filo cups are lightly browned. Allow them to cool briefly before serving.

e. Sweet Potato Pancakes with Lobster

After grating sweet potatoes and mixing with raw egg, seasoned salt, and a touch of cinnamon, shape the mixture into small patties and fry lightly on both sides. When finished, garnish with a dollop of sour cream and lobster that has been seared in butter.

f. Bruschetta

Cut French bread in one-inch slices and bake. While the bread is baking, dice tomatoes and mix them with course salt, pepper, chopped garlic, basil, and mozzarella. Cover the slightly crunchy bread with the tomato mixture, being careful not to heap it too high as tumbling tomatoes don't make ladies in couture too happy.

g. Deviled Eggs Topped with Caviar

I don't have to explain this, right? Just use enough caviar to give the egg a little color.

h. Minicrabcakes

i. Miniquiches

j. Fresh Fruit and Cheese Tray

I'm not a chef, and I'm terrible at measuring, so I hesitate to give actual recipes. Trust yourself a little. If you'd rather not, consult B. *Smith's Entertaining and Cooking for Friends* for ideas.

Other Simple Entertaining Ideas

1. The simple Sunday brunch
Sometimes when you visit Bedside Baptist, you can fellowship with other congregants in the early afternoon over delightful breakfast/lunch combinations.

2. Winterque
What better way to "beat the blahs" than to have a winter barbeque?

3. Father-son luncheon
Men need to bond, too!

4. Old-fashioned cocktail party
It never went out of style.

5. Masquerade party
All night you can monster mash at this fun bash. Whether you select an era to emulate (i.e., The Roaring Twenties—Harlem Renaissance Style) or simply leave the costume choices open to your guests, this event can be a blast. If thrown around Halloween, "hoax foods," such as orange-and-black striped ravioli (by Nuovo Pasta Pro-

ductions, 1-800-803-0033), and scary tunes, such as Michael Jackson's "Thriller" and Whodini's "Haunted House of Rock," will make guests forget their fears and eat and dance the night away.

6. Old-fashioned tea party

Dust off your china. Some traditions should never be forgotten.

High tea on a Saturday or Sunday afternoon is a wonderful break from the norm. It's a tradition that we borrowed from our friends across the pond, but we can easily give it an American flair. When accompanied by soft music or even a live jazz trio, this can be a distinctive, elegant event. Traditionally, high tea was served in the early afternoon, and food included heavier edibles such as crustless sandwiches, pâté, and petit fours, while low tea was served later in the day and included gourmet tidbits rather than larger meals.

Armed with these great ideas, you can plan your social calendar for the upcoming year. As they say in New Orleans, *"Laissez les bons temps roulez!"*

THE
PRENUPTIAL

The words *prenuptial agreement* can spark heated conversations, set tongues clucking, inspire grand elabora-
tion, and start teeth-sucking. As the private lives of
celebrities and socialites are becoming more public, the
masses are privy to details that before were virtually un-
known to us. Good or bad, we've become somewhat aware
of what prenuptial agreements are, but as the old adage
goes, a little bit of information can be dangerous. So let
Ivana enlighten you so that you can be better informed on
the subject.

It's now time for the disclaimer. Just because I married
an attorney does not mean that I am qualified to give legal
advice. I urge you to obtain legal counsel before considering any matter pertaining to contracts or any other legal

affair. Do you understand? Of course, you do. Ivana knows that you are smart.

The prenuptial agreement, also called a premarital agreement or an antemarital agreement, is a contract between two people who are planning to marry. This agreement or contract determines the rights each party has to each other's property during the marriage and after the unfortunate dissolution of the marriage. We'd all prefer that the latter not occur, but just in case it does, you need to be prepared. Prenuptial agreements grew in popularity during the 1800s, primarily to protect the property of heiresses, whose property, prior to the 1848 Married Women's Property Act, went to their husbands upon marriage. The rationale for using these agreements has evolved over time, and they are now used to protect more than wealthy young women. There are different types of premarital agreements: those that pertain to divorce and those that pertain to death. Of those that pertain to divorce, some deal with property brought into a marriage and others deal with property acquired during the marriage.

In a recent poll of women across the country, diverse reactions poured forth when asked their opinions of potential mates who would ask them to sign prenuptial agreements. Descriptions included words such as *careful, selfish, mistrusting, foolish, undesirable, honest, smart, realistic, scared, cautious, suspicious, manipulative, financially savvy, paranoid, self-centered, guilty, greedy, sneaky, powerful, mature, aggressive,* and *financially successful.* As indicated by the range of responses, many emotions are tied into people's feeling about these agreements. Despite the fact that all of the respondents were either current college students or college graduates, they recognized that sexism dictates that many men have higher earning power than women. With that in mind, some of these women said they would be willing to take on traditional gender roles if asked to sign a prenuptial agreement and stay at home.

A comfortably situated, Los Angeles–based MBA in her late forties said, "My spiritual beliefs lead me to believe that the man should be the head of the household. Because of that, I understand the true role of the submissive wife— it does not mean that you are less in any way, but an equal partner with the husband taking major responsibility. With this is mind, I think traditional roles are fine, but it is up to each couple—whatever works best for them."

A Delaware-based COO in her early thirties concurred. "After a career of working with children and young people, I have a sense of the importance of having the unique opportunity to be truly raised by your parents, not just co-exist with them through childhood."

Not every woman found this decision to be so palatable because some viewed signing a prenuptial agreement as requiring them to give up something.

A Philadelphia-based teacher in her mid-thirties felt that making such a compromise was a control tactic, and she refused to be controlled. She said that she didn't like the idea of beginning a relationship with doubts by having a potential spouse sign a prenuptial agreement.

A New York–based television producer seconded that idea, with a slight twist. She was in a serious relationship with an athlete who also had lucrative business dealings, and she said, "I'm not in favor of the prenup because it suggests that if the marriage fails, this is what will happen. I'm of the mind-set that marriage is a lifelong commitment, and I'd rather come up with an agreement of what we can do to make the union last . . . till death do us part! I do understand the concept of the prenup, though. It's something my man and I would really have to discuss." When asked if she would be willing to follow the traditional gender roles, she responded, "It's not ideal for me; however, I will put family first and find a nice common ground."

Other women considered the prenuptial agreement to be another form of insurance, just like car insurance. "In other areas of your life, you prepare for the worst," said a thirty-two-year-old marketing specialist and former White House intern. "You get car insurance. That doesn't mean you think you're going to have an accident, but if you do, it's there. You buy homeowner's and flood insurance. No, you don't think that there will be a tornado or avalanche, but if there is, you have insurance. Prenups, to me, are the same thinking."

Some women, like this thirty-something financial analyst, wanted the best of both worlds, but she was open to the idea of staying at home. "I'm in agreement as long as I have some freedom to maybe work part-time or do a little something outside of the home . . . I believe that children require a lot of time and attention. Additionally, the professional workplace can be so strenuous and time-consuming nowadays that I think, if possible, one of the partners should focus on keeping things straight at home and providing the appropriate home life."

An eighteen-year-old college student agreed with that, but with a twist. "This is a new age, and men and women are switching roles. Some men are staying home with the kids while the missus is away at work."

Let's throw another twist into the debate. What about when the shoe is on the other foot, and the woman is the one who comes from moneyed stock?

One Philadelphia-based divorcée in her late fifties said that her family acquired their wealth through real estate and she believed that, in her case, having a potential spouse sign a prenuptial agreement was smart because she could protect past investments and protect her child. Because she has had to be so cautious, she has, in the past, hidden her financial status from potential paramours because revealing it "would prove to be a barrier." At the same time, she wouldn't consider marrying a man with considerably less wealth because of the complications and different expectations that come when two different classes meet on the playing field of love.

Remember the thirty-something financial analyst? Her family amassed wealth through hard work in the pharmaceuticals industry in corporate America. She'd been raised with high standards and high expectations, which made dating somewhat difficult. When asked if she would consider marrying someone with considerably less wealth than she, she responded, "Not at this age. Maybe five years ago, my response might have been different, but then again maybe not." She, too, attempted to hide her financial status although she didn't think she'd done a great job at it. "Some men can be easily intimidated. Others may feel that you are only interested in material things, and still others have their own hidden agendas." She cited as an example a man who wanted her to purchase a car for him. "He seemed to equate love with material possessions," she remembered bleakly. She was appalled when he suggested that he would make a good "house husband."

Talk about turning the tables.

Incidentally, most of the female college students polled would not consider marrying someone with less wealth than they, but most would consider signing a prenuptial agreement if marrying someone wealthier than they. One Atlanta-based student kept her explanation simple, saying, "Unfortunately, people get divorced, and when this happens, [maintaining my lifestyle] should not be an issue."

Another college student based in Virginia commented, "When you are married, you may find yourself purchasing things under both your and your spouse's names, which in turn makes them half yours and half his. You may have things that you may want back, and without a prenuptial agreement, you may never see those items again."

Rather than view the prenuptial agreement as a trap, it should be regarded as a safeguard, especially when both parties have significant holdings. The agreements are accepted in all states, but lawmakers in some states such as California are coming under pressure to challenge some divorce rulings. Prenuptial agreements can be amended with the written consent of both parties, or canceled by the creation, signing, and notarization of a Release of Premarital Agreement document. A prenuptial agreement can also be set aside by a divorce judge if the judge suspects fraud, failure to disclose, unfairness, and failure of the less-moneyed party to be adequately represented by counsel.

In the case of death, the state in which the deceased resided is the final heir. That is, ownership of your property will revert to the state if there is no named heir or the named heir is unable to be located. That's why it is important to have a will. Just as there are laws pertaining to the distribution of property after death, each state has laws pertaining to the distribution of assets (and liabilities) after divorce. States such as Arizona, California, Idaho, Louisiana, Nevada, New Mexico, Texas, Wisconsin, and the territory of Puerto Rico abide by community property statutes, which allow for a fifty-fifty split of marital assets, except for gifts from third parties. That's why it's important to have a prenuptial agreement.

In many marriages, two parties come together with few assets, as they intend to work together to build their assets. One might not think that there is a need for a prenuptial agreement in this case, but there actually is. This was the case with Gary Wendt and Lorna Jorgenson Wendt, the couple who made news in 1997, when their pricey parting was splashed across newspapers around the country.

The two married in Wisconsin in 1965 and moved to Cambridge, Massachusetts, while Gary pursued an MBA at Harvard, which he completed in 1967. The ensuing eight years were spent in Texas, Florida, and Georgia, where Gary worked in real estate while Lorna raised their two daughters and managed household affairs. From 1975 to 1998, Gary worked at General Electric Capital, rising through the ranks from real estate finance manager to chief executive officer, a position he took in 1985. Meanwhile, Lorna served as the hands-on parent, driving in carpools and checking homework, and the ambassador-like wife, entertaining potential clients.

In short, she provided the stability at home that enabled him to be the lion out in the world. In 1995, he asked her for a divorce, offering her something between $8 million and $11 million, approximately 10 percent of his worth. Because Lorna managed the household and had access to the savings, investment, and checking accounts, she knew exactly how much wealth she and her husband had acquired over their thirty-year marriage. She determined that her input was worth more than a measly 10 percent, so she contested the settlement details, asking for 50 percent, but in 1998, she was awarded $20 million, or roughly 20 percent of their holdings.

It's difficult for us average Americans to feel sympathy when discussing such large numbers, but the core issue of this remains the same. As an equal partner in a relationship in which initially both parties had little, the assets should be divided equally. Lorna Jorgenson Wendt made a human capital investment in the case of her husband, but the work she did in the marriage was "invisible," so neither her husband nor the judge recognized that. This is why in 1998, she established the Equality in Marriage Institute (www.equalityinmarriage.org). Lorna is now a vocal advocate for prenuptial agreements because she believes that they can open honest dialogue between couples about assets, expectations, and things we hold in esteem.

One Philadelphia-based, forty-something woman regards the prenuptial agreement with a levelheadedness that is refreshing. Married to a physician, this woman doesn't find the general idea of the prenuptial agreement to be objectionable. She says that she might sign one, depending on the contents of the agreement. "If I were asked to be a stay-at-home mom, I probably would only sign the agreement if there were some kind of financial compensation for the loss of lifestyle, income, and ability to gain employment because of the time away from the employment arena." She, like Lorna Wendt, recognizes that she is losing valuable job experience by staying home and managing the household. While some people think of home time as vacation time, these two women know their worth, and they are the types of women who can advocate intelligently for themselves.

In other marriages, one party might hail from a more affluent background than the other. Or it may be the second marriage for the more financially secure spouse-to-be.

In these cases, prenuptial agreements are especially important. For proof of this, look at the case of the second Mrs. Trump.

When she and husband Donald split, Marla Maples reportedly received a divorce settlement of $2.5 million, a mere pittance when compared with my namesake's reported settlement of $10 million in cash, a $12 million estate in Connecticut, $350,000 annual alimony, a $4 million housing allowance, and $100,000 in annual child support for each of her three children fathered by Trump. When Marla married the mogul, the couple was settling in for parenthood. Although she signed a prenuptial agreement, she claims that she did not read it and that she signed it under duress. (If the less-moneyed spouse can claim ignorance and coercion, often the prenuptial agreement can be renegotiated. This was reportedly the case with actress Amy Irving, who finally received a $100 million settlement from Steven Spielberg.) The thing that can work in her favor is the tenet that the breadwinner must keep the less-moneyed spouse in the lifestyle to which he or she has grown accustomed.

Of course, the judge will take into consideration the length of time the marriage lasted. In states basing their marital law on British common law, such as Connecticut, New Jersey, New York, and Pennsylvania, other issues considered in granting divorce judgments are income or property brought to the marriage by each party, present value of property, income and earning capacity of each party (including education background, training, etc.),

debts and liabilities of the divorcing parties, custodial issues pertaining to children, age and physical/emotional
health of the parties, and any extent to which one party
deferred achieving his or her career goals during the marriage.

Other reasons why people may want prenuptial agreements are they wish to preserve the financial stability of
their children from previous marriages, they wish to grant
protection for the second spouse from the first spouse, and
they wish to maintain autonomy in a preexisting business.
In addition, in some second marriages or unions between
people who have already established themselves in the
careers, couples wish to waive their rights to financial
support in the event of a divorce. (This can serve as an in-
centive for couples to pursue their own careers and accumulate their own wealth during the marriage.) These
waivers can, however, be overruled if deemed unfair by a
judge (i.e., one person is in danger of applying for public
assistance).

Discussing the prenuptial agreement can be a touchy
thing for couples. Emotions can run high, and accusations
of mistrust can fly. In some cases, weddings have been
called off because the issue was raised. Discussing who
gets what in the event of a divorce is about as unromantic
as you can get, but still it must be discussed. A lot of people naively think that marriage is solely an emotional
arrangement. This is not so. It is also a financial contract.
We enter into all sorts of contracts for much smaller, rou-
tine matters such as purchasing cell phones or getting

hardwood floors refinished in our homes. Lorna Jorgenson Wendt might advise that we negotiate wisely for what is probably the biggest social arrangement of our lives. Both parties become fully aware of their rights, responsibilities, and obligations before the wedding. If drawn up together, the writing process can reinforce the ideals and goals you two have set forth, making the prenuptial agreement the blueprint for your planning. This point should be stressed by the spouse-to-be who is advocating for the agreement.

In another poll that I conducted with men, I was attempting to gauge the male perspective on prenuptial agreements. The following are their descriptions of wealthy women who would require their potential husbands to sign on the dotted line: *smart, mistrustful, insecure, cheap, nervous, careful,* and *shallow.* Not too different from the women's descriptions, huh? As I delved further, I unearthed a torrent of feelings about such a woman, but I can't say that the results were shocking.

A Colorado-based contract administrator said that a woman who would ask for such an agreement "majors in self-preservation, which, I feel, has no place in a marriage." Not surprisingly, he said that he would not sign a prenuptial agreement. "I believe marriage is to be entered into with the idea that it will last 'as long as you both shall live.' With that in mind, why would I agree to a prenuptial?"

A Maryland-based system support engineer added, "Although I am not wealthy, I don't believe I'd require a prenup. Prenups speak volumes about faith, trust, and real love."

Meanwhile, a thirty-five-year-old writer based in North Carolina would not be offended by such a request if it came from a wealthy woman he was dating. He would regard her as a businesswoman who knows her value. Because of her net worth, she could afford to be more complicated than a woman entering a marriage without as much financial stability. Taking the idea a step further, he considered what he would do if asked to sign a prenuptial agreement. "I would sign it. I'm not concerned about living off of her money. I'm grown, and I should be able to support myself."

An Atlanta-based director of business planning and analysis in his early forties concurred. Unthreatened by such a request, he said that he would sign the agreement "if that's what she needs to protect her wealth, which was accumulated before we met." He, too, would seek to protect his assets if marrying someone with considerably less wealth than he. "I should be entitled to keep all that I made prior to us getting together," he said. Her refusal to sign his agreement could result in the termination of their relationship.

A Philadelphia-based journalist, author, and legislative aide remembered a relationship with a CPA four years his junior gone awry because of financial issues. "I dated a woman who was considerably wealthier than I. I broke off that relationship when I found that she thought her wealth would allow her to mistreat/disrespect me. Wealth is not as important to me as respect. I left her for a pauper whom I came to love and respect, and eventually marry," he revealed. For him, wealth was not as important as respect. "I can generate my own wealth, and I prefer to do so." When asked if he would ever marry without a prenuptial agreement, he said that he would. "I wouldn't marry someone whose character I did not respect, so there would be no need for a prenuptial agreement."

Some men, like a Philadelphia-based talk radio host, prefer not to focus on thorny points like the prenuptial agreement. In his early forties, the radio pundit dated a pharmaceutical scientist two years his junior, whose income was significantly higher than his. When asked if he would sign a prenuptial agreement to marry her, he responded in the negative. "I would hope that going into the marriage, we would assume that it would last and that neither person is looking for any type of assurance or insurance."

Because so many women place high importance on a man's earning potential, some men have become insecure about the way they are viewed. The Colorado-based contract administrator asserted, "I'm not in dire straits financially, but I certainly don't make a point of making that known. I have always wanted to be seen as a person of value regardless of what someone thought I had, and I extended the same grace to others."

The North Carolina–based writer expounded on that

point. "It's hard to tell which women are interested primarily in a man's money. Some women are blatant with it, but the smart, conniving women are a more difficult read." Because of this fear, many men, like this writer, are careful about displaying their wealth because it can work to their detriment, not just with women but in people's perceptions in general. He said that he would end a relationship with a woman who seemed to have gold-digging tendencies or if her family regarded him as an ATM.

Most of the men surveyed said that they would consider marrying a woman with considerably less wealth than they possessed. "I could do it," Mr. North Carolina said, "but generally such a woman can't understand the value of saving. They'd think it's a lottery and they hit the jackpot." He would consider having such a woman sign a prenuptial agreement, but he would seek the advice of his lawyers first. Things that they'd discuss would include whether or not he'd been married before and what assets he had before the two solidified their relationship.

Those are smart steps to take, and they might go a long way in guarding against monetary mishaps in the marriage.

Now, let's move beyond the emotion and say that you are both willing to sign a prenuptial agreement. As you begin to prepare your prenuptial agreement, both of you will need to document financial statements (including potential inheritances, annual gross income, and interests in family trusts), a listing of real estate, and a listing of property owned individually (including pets, appliances, cars, etc.) and jointly. It's also important to remember to include assets such as pension plans as well.

The cost of preparing a prenuptial agreement can be minimal, if you decide to do it on your own—all you'll have to pay is the fee charged by the notary public—or cher, if an attorney is included and the document is intricate. Attorney Bridget Sullivan of Denver law firm Sherman and Howard, LLC, doesn't advise tackling the prenuptial agreement without an attorney. Some tips she gives are as follows:

1. Discuss the idea openly with as much detachment as possible. Don't make promises regarding specific terms before consulting an attorney because you don't want to get locked into anything prematurely.
2. Finalize prenuptial details far in advance of the wedding so that no one, feeling limited by little time before the wedding, can claim coercion.
3. Hire separate counsel.

With these tips in mind, broaching the subject of a prenuptial agreement can be relatively painless. Keep in mind that you are negotiating for your best interest and the best interests of the children that you will have as a married couple. If it is true love, your spouse-to-be will want you and your future offspring to be taken care of in life with or without him.

CLOSING
THOUGHTS

It has been my sincere hope in writing this book to provide you with some actual methods to meet and marry the Money Man of your dreams. The rationale behind my thinking is this: While money does not solve the world's problems, it sure as heck makes them a little more bearable, and its possession can insulate you from some troubling times and tough dilemmas that knock many of our less fortunate sisters off their feet.

It is my sincere hope that you find happiness in love because love is a wonderful thing. It's really the gift that God gives us with hopes that we will pass it on. We will pass it on to our Money Men, and the children we are blessed with caring for.

It is my sincere hope that after you've found happiness

in love and fortune in finances that you will use your time, energy, and money toward the betterment of your community and the world. In addition to establishing businesses to generate more wealth for themselves, many athletes have established foundations to help others. Others donate time at children's hospitals and shelters even when the cameras aren't rolling. Make sure that you do the same. Yeah, the charity balls are fun, but make sure that you are around when it comes time to do the hard work, too.

It is my sincere hope that you, Simone, Sharon, Cheniqua, and Sasha, have been inspired to reach for your dreams no matter what they are. Don't be afraid to claim the best for yourself because you are worth it. If what is best for you happens to be of little visible value to anyone else, Ivana included, that's okay. Take it, shape it, and make it into your purest reality.

Go for the gold!

—Ivana B. Rich